CONTINUITY
MODEL
GENERATION

CONTINUITY MODEL GENERATION

Integrating Wealth, Strategy, Talent, and Governance Plans

JUSTIN B. CRAIG, PhD

WILEY

For general information on our other products and services or for technical support, please contact our Customer Care Department within the United States at (800) 762-2974, outside the United States at (317) 572-3993 or fax (317) 572-4002.

Wiley also publishes its books in a variety of electronic formats. Some content that appears in print may not be available in electronic formats. For more information about Wiley products, visit our web site at www.wiley.com.

Library of Congress Cataloging-in-Publication Data is Available:

ISBN 978-1-119-75930-0 (Hardback)
ISBN 978-1-119-75935-5 (ePub)
ISBN 978-1-119-75929-4 (ePDF)

Cover image: © GETTY IMAGES | OXYGEN
Cover design: PAUL McCARTHY

SKY10030224_101221

| Strategic Planning for Continuity | **C** **A** | Successor Talent Planning for Continuity |

CONTINUITY

V

| Asset, Wealth, Estate Planning for Continuity | **A** **S** | Governance Planning for Continuity |

| Quadruple Bottom Line Scorecard | **C** **A** | Individual Philosophy of Stewardship |

CONTINUITY

V

| Personal Legacy Statement | **A** **S** | Family Governance Philosophy |

Contents

Contents

List of Illustrations

List of Illustrated Tables

List of Configuration Plans

Acknowledgments and Appreciation

First, I respectfully acknowledge the family of business-owning families worldwide who have taught and inspired me, and countless contemporaries, through their commitment to establishing models that ensure future generations continue to make significant social and economic impacts. Thanks for allowing me to stalk you!

Second, to those whose thinking, testing, pivoting, and retesting have contributed to my ability to interpret and share the 21 frameworks and bring them together as the Continuity Canvas. I am fortunate to have worked closely with several of the family enterprise field's pioneers over the past two decades. Notable amongst these are my two main mentors (and mates), Professors Emeriti Ken Moores and John Ward. These two gentle men have more in common than they know. . .And I know that because I have been fortunate enough to spend countless hours learning at their feet. Ken and John, I hope this book brings your thinking to a new generation of family enterprise zealots, and I'll do my best to ensure it does. Your fingerprints are all over these pages.

I also need to tip my hat, in no particular order, to the colleagues and practitioners who have helped craft my thinking and enflame my passion for family enterprise. To the Dennis family for sharing your journey with me for the past two decades; thank you for the Four Rs as well as the Church and State framework. To the Urrea family, who have recently brought additional texture and sophistication to the Church and State approach to governance. To the Millers for their amazing work with the Four Cs framework. . . truly groundbreaking. To Professor Ivan Lansberg, whose eloquent portrayal of the Four Tests is timeless. To the pioneering Professor John Davis and late Renato Taiguiri, who gifted us such a sound foundation through the Three Circles paradigmatic framework. To my friend Professor Jose Liberti, who enlightened me on the four ways to capture value. To Jim Davis and his colleagues for introducing me and others to stewardship as a theory. To Jim Ethier for helping me understand what Governance Planning really means. And to Drew Everett, who helped me appreciate the meaning of Successors' Talent development. To the Lee family, for allowing me to understand the true meaning of sibling partnership. And to the many families who helped me understand the true meaning of long-term orientation and stewardship.

A separate acknowledgement to friends who have helped me more than they know. To Dr. Dennis Jaffe for his guidance along my trip to now. Dennis was instrumental in getting me started and keeping me going. It was he who provided the final push and the invaluable recommendation to Wiley. And to Caroline Coleman Bailey and her network at the innovative Premier Growth organization. And last but far from least, to Professors Eric Clinton and Catherine Faherty as well as their Irish family business community at Dublin City University. Much of what you will read in the pages that follow was tested for its final 'proof of concept' with Eric's, Catherine's, and Caroline's learning communities.

To my friends in the professional services community, thank you for helping me to appreciate your important role more fully, and for helping me discover more than just the many moving parts of estate, wealth, and asset planning. In particular, I thank Bruce Hatcher from BDO Australia and Jonathan Flack and Jay Mattie from PwC US. Their passion for genuine understanding has motivated many advisors and subsequently helped countless business-owning families.

I also owe a ridiculously huge debt of gratitude to several people I have never actually met, but whose work I have long admired, "borrowed from," and paraphrased in these pages. Specifically, to Dr. Ichak Adizes, whose understanding of life cycle is without peer; to Professor Emeritus Robert Kaplan and David Norton for sharing their Balanced Scorecard with me and the world; to Professor Sara Sarasvathy, whose work introducing effectual reasoning has made the complex simpler for so many of us; and to the global community of trust researchers whose work in understanding trust (within, between, and among teams of decision-making teams in family enterprises) underpins everything.

And finally, to my many colleagues at the institutions I have had the privilege to serve. To those who were with me at Oregon State University, Northeastern University in Boston, the Kellogg School of Management at Northwestern University, Dublin City University, and at my alma mater, Bond University. And to other colleagues including Professors Tom Lumpkin, Clay Dibrell, Don Neubaum, and Scott Newbert, who have pushed and challenged me along my anything-but-typical academic journey. And to Catharina Jecklin and Anke Steinmeyer, two doctoral students at Bond University, who represent an exciting new generation of thinkers.

You are all responsible for the *Continuity Model Generation*. Indeed, these pages harness my intellectual restlessness, which you all have tolerated and nurtured, and for that I am deeply grateful.

Justin

Introduction to the
Continuity Model Generation

This book is intentionally modelled on Wiley Publication's *Business Model Generation,* written by Alexander Osterwalder and Professor Yves Pigneur and co-created by an amazing crowd of 470 practitioners from 45 countries.

What is significant, and not widely comprehended, is that the *Business Model Generation* is actually about a movement. . . a generation. This movement has been insanely successful as it captured a generation that pined for, and subsequently related to, a refreshing way of thinking and acting. They evolved from the Business Plan Generation.

The *Continuity Model Generation* has morphed in a similar way. Seeking a refreshing approach, this generation of scholars and practitioners from across the globe evolved from the Succession Plan Generation.

For the Business Model Generation there are nine building blocks that form the basis for "a handy tool," i.e. the Business Model Canvas.

For the *Continuity Model Generation* there are 6 robust meta-frameworks, made up of 21 stress-tested frameworks with a total of 87 dimensions that form the foundation for the development of 4 "essential for continuity" planning processes, each with 4 segments and a nuanced cornerstone concept. These combine to deliver a tool, which is also very handy. We, the continuity model generation, unashamedly call this the Continuity Canvas.

Welcome to the movement.

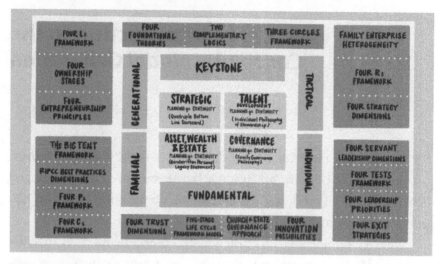

Illustration 1 21–6–4×4

Twenty-one frameworks, six meta-frameworks and four plans, each with four components. . . It all fits on a napkin!

Let the learning and creating begin. . .

Part I

21 Frameworks
and 6 Meta-Frameworks

Keystone Meta-Framework

Knowledge of this meta-framework's keystone, four theoretical approaches, two logics, and three circles will enable anyone to understand and interpret with some authority the complexity of the tripartite family, business, and ownership landscape as well as gain insight into how these areas function independently and interdependently.

Four Foundational Theoretical Approaches

Agency Theory

Agency theory explains so much of the world. Originating in arguments presented as early as 1932, agency theory describes what happens when owners appoint others to act on their behalf—or, in the theoretical jargon, when principals appoint agents. The core argument is that any organization, at some point, will reach a stage, due to growth or expansion, where the principal cannot do everything that needs to be done, so they must appoint someone to do some of the work. This eventuality brings about or facilitates a cost: the person, or agent, appointed by the principal to act on their behalf will require monitoring, which incurs agency costs, also known as monitoring costs. As a leader of a third-generation European family enterprise shared insightfully, "My sole job is to reduce agency costs."

Broadly, then, the job of a leader is to put in place mechanisms in the organization to ensure that agents' behavior is aligned with interests of the principals. This alignment is achieved through incentives and perquisites.

Importantly, agency costs occur throughout an organization. At the organization's head, agency costs appear when the owners appoint the board to act on their behalf. The board is monitored through measures such as the strategic planning process and other governance-related and regulatory mechanisms to ensure those appointed by the owners truly act on their behalf. This is predominant in publicly traded companies but is also the case for private companies, particularly in mature generational businesses with more complex governance structures.

Moreover, one of the responsibilities of the board of directors is to appoint and monitor the CEO. Agency costs, or the potential for agency costs, will occur if the CEO's actions, decisions, or behaviors are not aligned with those of the board of directors, who are acting as representatives of the owners.

Moving down through the organization, there are also potential agency costs when the CEO appoints their management team. This potential eventuates if those top executives are not aligned amongst themselves.

If you keep the thread going, further down the organization the senior management team is charged with overseeing different areas, be it marketing, finance, IT, logistics, sales, or others. Again, there is potential for agency costs in misalignment of the senior management team with those appointed as division leaders or department heads.

These middle managers or supervisors, in turn, will employ line staff, resulting in yet another principal–agent dyad, and the potential for more agency costs.

As such, an organization represents a chain of principals and agents, with the same individuals or entities taking on either role, depending on the dyad relationship in question. Recall, at the top of the organization, the principal was the owner, and the board was the agent; then the board was the principal, and the CEO was their agent; then the CEO was the principal, and their agent was the top management team. The top management team members then represent the principal in their dyadic relationship with their line employees. And so on.

So, as should be evident, agency costs, or the potential for agency costs, are ubiquitous throughout all organizations. It is for this reason that agency is one of the frameworks in the keystone meta-framework.

Family enterprises are not immune to agency costs, or the potential for agency costs. They too incur costs throughout the organization and the family. In the early days, the owners are also the managers, so there is a reduction of agency-related costs. But as the company evolves and the family grows, the owners typically must appoint non-family employees and managers to assist in operations and non-family directors to assist in governance. Family and non-family members will contribute to the potential for agency costs if they are not aligned with the values, beliefs, or vision of the core ownership group.

In family enterprises there are four specific categories of agency costs. The first category is probably the most common and easiest to comprehend: *entrenchment*. Here, a founder, or any senior executive or other employee becomes entrenched in their position and their way of doing things. This happens not only in the domain of business-owning families, but, typically, entrenchment-related agency costs will be incurred if a senior executive or, particularly, an incumbent leader is not willing to succeed responsibility to the next generation and stays too long in their role. These costs relate to being wedded to old ways and the unwillingness to embrace change and innovation, which, paradoxically, were likely the hallmarks of the executive's earlier leadership and a major reason for their success.

The second theoretical dimension related to agency costs is *adverse selection*. This effectively says that the best person for a given job or position should be appointed regardless of whether that individual is family or non-family. As is the case for non-family businesses as well, there is a large potential to incur agency costs should the wrong person be appointed, such as when nepotism is involved.

The third agency-cost-related category relates to *information asymmetry*. Here, there will be cost incurred, or the potential for costs, if information is kept from people who should be given access to it or used inappropriately by those with access. For example, information asymmetry manifests in the form of insider trading in publicly traded companies, when someone who has access to superior information acts on that information to benefit themselves at the company's expense. This type of cost is potentially rife in family enterprises where those working for the business in day-to-day operations or in executive roles have access to information that those not working in the business lack. It also manifests in boards, when a board member has access to information others do not and acts on that information in an inappropriate way.

Finally, the potential for agency costs is also associated with *altruism*. Here the problem can be that all family members will be treated equally—such as offered the same compensation or similar-level business roles—despite their divergent contributions to the business or the family in governance or other roles. This is a recipe for disaster.

To recap, entrenchment is when incumbents overstay their welcome, preventing effective succession; adverse selection is also known as nepotism and causes problems when family members are appointed to positions for which they are not qualified; information asymmetry, also known as insider trading in publicly traded companies, denotes situations where access to superior information is used inappropriately; and altruism, in this context, involves treating everyone equally regardless of what they contribute (Illustration 2).

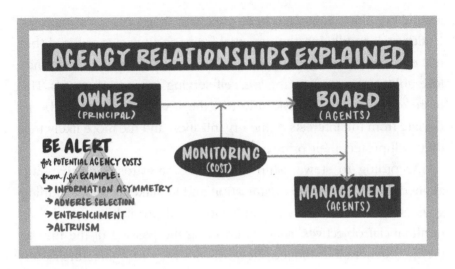

Illustration 2 AGENCY

Achievement of continuity requires understanding and minimiz-
ing agency-related costs. One way to do that is through the Continuity Canvas's four essential plans. A fundamental continuity model
concept, and a key way to reduce agency costs, is to ensure that
agents act as stewards, as we discuss next.

Stewardship Theory

Stewardship theory defines relationships based on behavioral prem-
ises not addressed by the principal–agent interest divergence that
agency theory poses. According to stewardship theory, agents' objectives can be aligned with those of the organization, and the utility gained through pro-organizational behaviors is higher than those
gained through individualistic, self-serving behaviors.

If the agent is intrinsically motivated, they will most likely design
an organizational setting where higher-order needs are encouraged
and fostered. In an effort to pursue these higher-order needs, agents
will be motivated to work harder on behalf of the organization,

a condition that aligns their behaviors with their principals' interests. Under such conditions, the potential for opportunism is reduced (but not eliminated) as agents gain little or no utility (and, in fact, may lose utility) by pursuing tangible, self-serving economic rewards. The more agents value intrinsic rewards, the less likely they will be to deviate from the interests of the organization and the more likely that they will protect their principals' interests.

According to stewardship theory, the stewards' objectives are aligned with those of the organization and its stakeholders, including goals such as sales growth, innovation, and profitability as well as nonfinancial objectives, such as ensuring the passing of the firm to the next generation. Indeed, stewards not only recognize their obligation to protect the interests of the organization but also believe that they are morally obligated to pursue them.

According to Jim Davis, David Schoorman, and Lex Donaldson, the authors of the seminal stewardship work (Davis, Schoorman, and Donaldson 1997), stewardship can be characterized by six interrelated dimensions: intrinsic motivation, organizational identification, use of personal forms of power, collectivism, low power distance, and involvement orientation (Illustration 3). They propose that, unlike agency theory, which emphasizes economic rationality, the concept of stewardship captures other-focused, prosocial non-economic behaviors. More specifically, in contrast to agency-based situations, where extrinsic, tangible, and exchangeable commodities are used to motivate and reward employees, a stewardship-based environment will emphasize intrinsic rewards that foster intrinsic motivation, such as opportunities for personal growth and achievement, affiliation, and self-actualization. To fulfill these higher-order needs, stewards' intrinsic motivation will push them to work harder on behalf of the organization, which in turn aligns their behaviors with their principals' interests. Generally, stewards will work harder to achieve the organization's goals when they believe their work is meaningful and their tasks are significant.

Organizational practices that emphasize employee growth and signal managerial support to employees can provide stewards with the rewards they seek and nurture their intrinsic motivation.

Another key distinction of stewardship is that it fosters members who identify with the organization and view it as an extension of themselves. According to Davis et al. (1997, p. 29), "identification occurs when managers define themselves in terms of their membership in a particular organization by accepting the organization's mission, vision, and objectives." Stewards, therefore, have a strong sense of attachment to their organizations, possess high levels of psychological ownership, and wish to see their organizations succeed. Relatedly, stewards have a psychological preference for using personal power instead of institution-based forms of power. Rather than flowing from formally established authority, personal power stems from interpersonal relationships, is often built over time, and is based on mutual trust, norms of reciprocity, and information exchange.

From an organizational—as opposed to individual—level, stewardship directs behavior toward enhancing the collective good. A collectivist organization emphasizes the accomplishment of organizational goals, and individuals define themselves as part of the organization, one in which group identity and a sense of belonging reign supreme. That is, organizations with a stewardship climate are more likely to emphasize collectivism over individualism.

Such organizations are also identifiable by low power distances between managers and subordinates. Power distance is the extent to which less powerful members of an organization accept an unequal distribution of power across organizational levels. In organizational settings characterized by a high power distance, people with less power are dependent on those with high power and status, and special privileges are given to those with higher rank. Conversely, in organizations with low power distances, processes and interactions are egalitarian, inequalities are discouraged, and members are treated equally.

Finally, stewardship engenders a high involvement orientation. High-involvement work practices expand employee autonomy and involvement in decision-making processes and produce beneficial results for organizations and their employees. For example, such systems offer employees the chance to expand their knowledge and task-level expertise, involve people across levels in important organizational processes, and link individual performance to organizational outcomes. Reward systems are linked to performance in a way that instills individuals with the desire to accomplish organizational goals. Such involvement-oriented management environments, in which people are enabled to reach their potential and awarded increasing responsibilities and challenges, are consistent with a stewardship orientation and with the pursuit of aligning individual and organizational objectives.

We can plot the six dimensions of stewardship on a series of continua. For example, motivation can be anchored by extrinsic at one end and intrinsic at the other. For culture, it is collectivist and individual; power distance is high versus low; involvement orientation is involved versus detached; power is positional versus personal; the extent to which individuals view the business as an extension of themselves is high versus low. It is important to note that each of these dimensions, depicted through the series of continua, do not represent an either–or, or all–or–none, situation. For example, someone is not either intrinsically or extrinsically motivated; they will fall somewhere along that dimension. Thus, we can better understand stewardship by recognizing that a recommended position along a given continuum leans toward the preferred stewardship characteristic end.

Integrating the stewardship and agency arguments, or theoretical perspectives, we can suggest that it is preferred that agents appointed by principals are stewards. Below we embellish this further with the addition of the steward, or the concept of stewardship, to the three circles framework.

Without giving too much away, but as a way to reinforce the conceptualization of agents as stewards, continuity modelling is predicated on the notion that owners need to be stewards, that families need to be stewards, and that managers need to be stewards, who are more likely to: be intrinsically motivated, see the business as an extension of themselves, and use personal rather than positional power in companies characterized by collectivist cultures, low power distances, and a strong involvement orientation.

If being a steward is at one end of a continuum, what is at the other? It was only recently that I have begun to figure this out. The inverse to being a steward is being a corporate psychopath. This may sound confronting, and it is. The characteristics of a corporate psychopath, as defined in the psychology literature, can easily be accessed, and this is encouraged if you, like me, were wanting to better understand others who thrived in plain sight, even though their behaviors were so contrary to others in the system. A cursory review of this literature will reveal that while the word "psychopath" is a popular one, it's a colloquial term, not a medical one. The technical

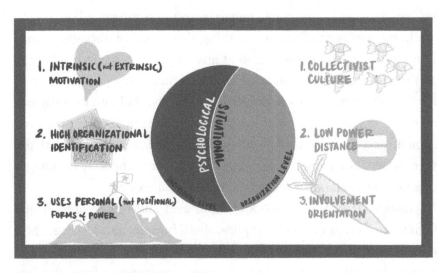

Illustration 3 STEWARDSHIP

diagnosis that appears in the *Diagnostic and Statistical Manual of Mental Disorders* is "antisocial personality disorder." A closer investigation will reveal that psychopathy is one of three traits that make up what the personality psychologists refer to as the Dark Triad, with narcissism and Machiavellianism being the others.

Resource-Based View

The resource-based view (RBV) of the firm suggests that firms survive based on their ability to combine heterogeneous and imperfectly mobile resources. Broadly, the RBV incorporates the complex, idiosyncratic, and unique nature of a firm's internal processes and intangible assets, including the values, beliefs, symbols, and interpersonal relationships that individuals or groups within the firm possess. As such, the RBV focuses on an analysis of the nature, characteristics, and potential of a firm's resource base and assumes that each firm's internal resources and capabilities are heterogeneous, which ultimately delivers a competitive advantage. Barney (1991) identified that in order to contribute optimally to firm sustainability, resources must be valuable, rare, imperfectly imitable, and non-substitutable (VRIN).

Resources are defined as anything that could be thought of as a firm's strength or weakness and at any given time could be defined as those (tangible and intangible) assets tied semi-permanently to the firm. Firm resources in the RBV perspective fall into four capital-related categories: physical capital, human capital, organizational capital, and process capital. Overcoming newness means that the venture has been able to distinguish itself from others by building a unique combination of resources in these categories.

Using the RBV framework, Sirmon and Hitt (2003) argued that family businesses evaluate, acquire, shed, bundle, and leverage their resources in ways that are different from those of non-family businesses. In part, these unique resources can emerge from the fact that family members often also act as owners and/or managers. In the family business context, the term "familiness" defines the unique bundle of idiosyncratic resources and capabilities that family firms hold (Habbershon and Williams, 1999). As such, familiness is one of the intangible factors in the RBV (Illustration 4).

Identifying the resource categories that are idiosyncratic is only part of the process. As, if not more important, is understanding *what* the firm does with resource-related processes or actions. Effectively managing the resources is crucial to creating a competitive advantage and this requires an understanding of how resources are accumulated, bundled, and leveraged. More specifically, Sirmon and colleagues consider resource management to include *structuring* (i.e. acquiring, accumulating, and divesting) the portfolio of resources, *bundling* (i.e. stabilizing, enriching, and pioneering) resources to build capabilities, and *leveraging* (i.e. mobilizing, coordinating, and deploying) capabilities in the marketplace. The synchronization of these processes is important to create value and, in the context of this conversation, contribute optimally to continuity.

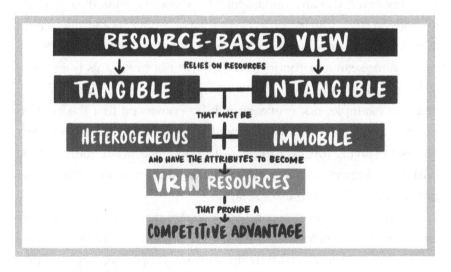

Illustration 4 RESOURCE-BASED VIEW

Principal Cost Theory

An additional, very useful component in the theoretical understanding of family enterprises, and how they improve the chances of continuity, is principal cost theory (Goshen and Squire 2010).

The two major cost dimensions or components of principal cost theory are *conflict* and *competence* (Illustration 5). The argument here is something that has long been overlooked: that there are costs in the appointment of principals. Where these costs manifest in the continuity model generation perspective is when owners are ill-prepared for the responsibility of ownership. This is also the case for directors, but that is covered largely by the agency cost argument. Regardless, understanding or appreciating that owners are potentially compromising their potential by falling victim to one or both of these principal costs characteristics is important.

Like many of the dimensions included in the 21 frameworks, the dimensions of conflict and competence are easy to interpret, remember, and explain. These two dimensions and how they apply in family enterprise are fundamental for those committed to continuity. Indeed, the primary objective as a continuity model generation member is to do whatever it takes to put the family enterprise in position for seamless continuation. That is not to say this is a simple task and there won't be plenty of opportunity to engage in conflict. For example, not everyone will be convinced that the conversation should move from traditional succession planning to a new mindset evolving toward *Continuity Model Generation;* there will be pushback. Expecting this pushback and framing it in terms of the principal cost is a simple solution.

Similarly, confusion around the concept of competence is likely and should be anticipated. The solution lies in explaining that costs will be incurred in the ownership group if people are not prepared for the responsibilities of ownership. This does not point the finger

Illustration 5 PRINCIPAL COST

at any one person but alerts the collective of the issue, which can be addressed through education and communication. In reality, this is not a hard sell. As will become more evident throughout this book, *Continuity Model Generation* proponents seek a fresh, unifying approach to reduce conflict and tension within, between, and among stakeholders in the family enterprise system. This conflict and tension, in principal–cost theoretical terms, is explainable through the dimensions of (i) conflict of interest, and (ii) individual competency, both of which can be addressed through systematic education and communication.

Two Complementary Logics

One simple way to understand what's different about family enterprises is to consider that they are driven by two complementary logics. Specifically, they pursue economic and social agendas concurrently. They balance doing well and doing good. They are committed to a healthy business with a long-term perspective characterized by patient capital and at the same time dedicated to contributing to the social wellbeing of their family, employees, and the communities in which they operate. Understanding this keystone characteristic is important for the development of a continuity model mindset.

Again, this is not hard to understand, and for some it may even sound overly simplistic. But in order to set a solid foundation and to educate now- and next-generation members, simple messages are the best. By framing the distinction as two complementary logics—those associated with economic and social agendas—you can share a simple, easily understood "story." Simple stories are best. It is also possible to draw this distinction to explain something vital. The way I like to do this is by drawing two connected circles, one with a heart and the other with a dollar sign. That picture paints more than a thousand words, leaving nothing more to be said. I encourage you to test this approach. Actually, throughout the book you'll find simple-to-replicate images that bring the ideas here to life effectively and efficiently. None are simpler than this one (Illustration 6).

But to understand the logics concepts even further, consider two exemplars of them: S.C. Johnson and Corning.

Samuel C. Johnson, then-fourth-generation leader of S.C. Johnson, captures his firm's economic and social motivations in his collection of essays to celebrate the company's one-hundred-year anniversary in 1986. He writes, "when family ownership places a family member in control of a company, and everyone in the firm knows clearly who the boss is, and who will still be the boss in five or ten years hence, then there's a palpable air of stability" (Johnson 1988, p. 7). The Johnsons expect brave decision-making by their generational leaders and have a proud history of each generation bringing something new to the enterprise: "that is, something that hadn't been thought of by—and beyond the visions of—the previous generations" (Johnson 1988, p. 8). At the same time, S.C. Johnson's leaders are acutely aware that they serve under the watchful eye of the founders. As Sam Johnson pointed out, family companies have the capacity to "do things of social or cultural value that a public company might be reluctant even to entertain," as they have the discretion to "do those things to contribute to enhance the communities in which we live and work without having to explain it to thousands and thousands of people over and over" (Johnson 1988, p. 13).

The social and economic interplay manifests in the US city of Racine, Wisconsin, home of the S.C. Johnson organization. A recent visit confirmed the prominence of the Johnson family in the town; beyond core business activities, other commercial operations include the Johnson Financial Group, the Johnson Bank, and Johnson Outdoors. There is also Sam Johnson Parkway, which leads to a Johnson-funded public square. The Johnson family has also endowed the Racine Museum of Art.

Another example is in the city of Corning, New York, home of the fifth-generation Houghton family's Corning Glass Works, where family connections and values account for much of the business's character and culture, with a focus on the social and economic well-being of the firm and its environment. When floodwaters destroyed the glassworks in 1972 and threatened the continuity of the business, then-Chairman Amory Houghton went on local radio to rally the company and community, "We are not only going to rebuild what we have lost, but we are going to add significantly to our manufacturing facilities in one of our plants. . .I want those of you who are employees of our company to know that as long as we respond well to our customer's needs your jobs are secure. Not a flood, nor a hurricane, not any other act of nature is going to jeopardize this. You are the Corning Glass Works, particularly in this city which is our home and our headquarters" (Dyer and Gross, 2001, p. 313).

Most notable is the positioning of continuity as the family's metric of success. By positioning this as their desired outcome and highlighting the economic and social aspects of achieving this, they acknowledge the role that their business families play in commerce and society.

Illustration 6 TWO COMPLEMENTARY LOGICS

Three Circles Framework

The three circle Venn diagram is synonymous with family enterprising and, as a go-to model since the mid-1980s, has reached consensus as a paradigm in this space. Much has been written about the three circles model, and a quick Google™ search will return plenty of variations on it (I encourage you to do that search). But while there are many variations, the overall message remains the same: that there are three independent *and* interdependent circles in family enterprise, and these circles are in constant flux, which helps explain the complexities and challenges that those involved in enterprising families face.

Like many easy-to-digest frameworks, the simplicity of the three circles model masks its complexity. Indeed, few in my experience have taken the time to appreciate the richness and explanatory power of this framework. Allow me to share my interpretation. But "my" is a mischaracterization, because the way I view the world has been influenced by many, as I explained in the Acknowledgements.

As with other frameworks, to really appreciate the three circles you need to draw it. So, do that: actually, take a piece of paper and draw three equal-sized intersecting circles. Label the circles "family," "owners," and "managers." The reason the third is labeled "managers" and not "business" is that the former keeps the level of analysis the same across circles; they are all people. This may seem pedantic, but it really is the best way to explain the interaction of these three systems. I will call them "systems" for ease of interpretation, though many purists would argue that they are not in fact systems. That conversation is beyond this book's scope.

So, now on the paper in front of you, there should be three circles denoting family, owners, and managers. The order of the labels doesn't matter. However, I have heard that the pioneers of this approach prefer to put the owners in the top circle because, in their words, "the ownership system overrules both the family and the managers system." But that conversation, too, is a distraction. The owner and family labels are easy to understand. The manager label takes some getting used to. To repeat, the managers are people as opposed to businesses, which are not people, though obviously operated by people. Managers manage on behalf of the owners, some, but not all, of whom will be in management. This is the fundamental distinction.

Now let's look at each of the systems/circles individually. Concentrate first on the owner circle. As a truly committed continuity model generation member, the first thing you need to do is add the word "stewards" to the word "owners." So you have a new label, "owners–stewards." Straightaway you have shifted the focus to continuity. Do the same for the other two circles/systems, adding "stewards" to their labels. Your Venn diagram now looks different. The simple relabeling of the three circles to include the word "stewards" makes the model more in line with the concept of continuity.

Back to the ownership circle, or more correctly, the owners–stewards system. What needs to be understood here, as you appreciate the richness of this model, is that there is heterogeneity within the ownership–stewardship system: different owners interpret their role as owners, and the utility that they receive from being owners, differently. So, while it is easy to simply relabel the system "owners–stewards," this won't necessarily be interpreted similarly by the increasing number of individuals in the ownership system.

What continuity modelers do to explain the complexity of ownership is to draw a continuum. So, include a continuum in the owners–stewards circle. The anchors of this continuum, and here we borrow from the complementary logics argument introduced earlier, are a dollar sign and a heart. Or, more specifically, you may prefer to describe these as economic utility and psychological utility. Regardless, understand that not all owners are the same, so they can be plotted along this continuum; importantly, where they are located will change over time. Also understand that this is not abnormal. This is normal. The beauty of approaching the three circles diagram with this granularity is that it shines a light on the systems both individually and collectively. By simply understanding that owners will not be the same, that they will have different needs and expectations, is enlightening. Some will be there primarily for the dividends; others will be there for the psychological and emotional attachment that they have to the family brand, to the clan, to the reputation. It will vary by degrees. But it will almost certainly vary.

The continuity model approach, as will be demonstrated throughout this book, is more expansive than many of the other approaches most readers will be familiar with. The idea explained above, of using the ownership system to include the concept of owners–stewards and broadening understanding of the utility gained by individual owners, is a good example of this expansiveness. Hopefully, this first example will prepare you to expand your horizons in other ways, such as appreciating the differences between continuity modeling and succession planning, as we'll discuss.

Before leaving the owners–stewards system, let's consider other ways to make use of this fundamental dimension of family enterprising. Continuity modelers are knowledgeable about, but not obsessed by, what it is that they actually own (as we'll discuss in Part II, which covers the development of the Continuity Canvas). Using the owners–stewards circle to illustrate, consider for this exercise what it is that you own: what you own collectively (with others), individually, in joint venture relationships, in partnerships, or in legal entities such as discretionary trusts. Any conversation on these topics would be housed in the owners–stewards circle. At this point, I'll assume that you appreciate more fully the richness of this first of three systems, more so than before you started this exercise. So, as not to overwhelm, let's move to the family circle, which you should now consider the family–stewards circle.

Like the other circles or systems in the model, this one is in flux. But this is the system that distinguishes business families or family enterprises from other entities. Other entities have to worry only about ownership and what it is that they are responsible to manage. Importantly, the family–stewards system evolves into a family of families. That simple framing is important. The best way to describe that, or depict it figuratively, is by including smaller circles within the larger one you've drawn. You now have something that resembles a simple polka dot image. If only the underlying dynamics were that simple!

In contrast, the family of families is susceptible to many unforeseen and challenging events. Indeed, the contemporary family itself is hard to describe. As someone once said about family offices, "If you've seen one family office you have seen one family office"; but the same can be said about families. They are all the same but different, and each family must learn to understand and manage what makes it different from others. This is a challenge, to be sure. But this is not the place to examine in detail and categorize carefully the diverse family makeups across society; rather, here we will flag that a focus on continuity will involve an understanding that the family in family enterprise represents a convoluted, ever-changing dynamic. For example, there are societal norm challenges in the Western world based on different views of marriage than those of the previous generation; the official recognition of same-sex marriages and partnerships has challenged the previously held definition of "family". Add to that the reality that a considerable proportion of marriages end in divorce, yielding many more single-parent and hybrid families than in the past, and the idea of labeling the system as family–stewards seems admittedly simplistic and idealistic.

But ultimately that doesn't matter. What matters is that no matter what constellation of family makeups constitute the family–stewards system, the focus is on ensuring that there is unity of purpose. Fostering a commitment to engage meaningfully with one another for the purpose of increasing chances of continuity: that's the right message to send those who populate whatever form or structure that constitutes the evolving family of families. Again, it is important to emphasize that a cursory examination of the three systems that make up the traditional family enterprise Venn diagram would not have elicited such richness.

Let's move now to the third system: the managers–stewards, or those who manage on behalf of the owners–stewards. In the owners–stewards system, my suggestion was that you draw a continuum bounded at one end with a heart and the other a dollar sign, or labeled "financial" and "psychological." In the family–stewards circle I encouraged you to draw smaller family units within the larger family system. In the manager–stewards circle I suggest the addition of a series of bullet points. This will enable a list of what it is that manager–stewards must manage. The list will include, for example, the operating business (sometimes called the legacy business), real estate holdings, liquid assets, philanthropic activities, joint ventures, and the like. The older and more established the business, the more bullet points that are likely to be included in this system. As with the other two systems, this modification adds a level of detail that helps you understand and appreciate how this simple framework can be used to tell such a complex story.

And that is the key message for all of these frameworks: they are a simple way to tell complex stories.

So, in front of you now should be three circles with edited labels and continuums, circles, and bullet points. The next step is to form the circles into dyads, to look at the framework in yet another way. But there is no need to draw a revised set of circles. Rather, just focus on one pairing of circles at a time. First, consider the overlap between the owners and managers. The argument here, and a key component of the approach we will use to build the Continuity Canvas in Part II, is that there is tension, or the potential for tension, between the managers–stewards and the owners–stewards. Recall that the managers–stewards manage on behalf of the owners–stewards. What is required to reduce the potential for conflict or tension is a strategic plan to ensure alignment between these two groups. As will be shown in Part II, this is one of four essential plans that make up the Continuity Canvas. We use the same approach, not surprisingly, at the intersection of the owners–stewards and family–stewards systems. In this dyad, we address the potential for tension through development of an asset, wealth, and estate plan. Moving to the overlap between the family–stewards and the managers–stewards system, to address the potential for tension between these two systems requires a successors' talent development plan. Finally, at the center of the three systems, where the three circles overlap, there is again potential for tension. To reduce this tension, or its potential, and increase the likelihood of continuity, the *Continuity Model Generation* commits to the development and implementation of a governance plan.

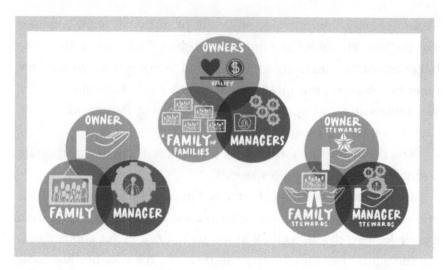

Illustration 7 FULLY DEVELOPED THREE CIRCLES FRAMEWORK

As stated earlier, the simplicity of the three circles framework masks its richness. While previous generations have acknowledged that the paradigm is useful in distinguishing what is unique to business-owning families, the *Continuity Model Generation* extends a level of sophistication to this framework, as suggested in the sections above (Illustration 7).

Upon adding the three circles framework to the four foundational theories (agency, stewardship, resource-based view, and principal cost) as well as to the complementary logics (economic and social) approach, it is apparent why this meta-framework is the keystone in the arch of continuity modeling. Feel free to reread this section and add your voice.

Familial Meta-Framework

While there is a familial component to everything for the *Continuity Model Generation*, the four frameworks within the familial meta-framework make difficult conversations much easier.

The Big Tent Framework

As businesses and families evolve, promoting meaningful involvement and engagement among enterprise members presents a challenge. As one sage family business leader suggests, "entitlement and wealth become the enemy."

Most families that have effectively addressed the challenge of engagement pursue a big tent approach. It's the idea that family leaders prefer to have the growing number of family members inside the tent, where they are provided appropriate education and other development support for meaningful roles, rather than outside the tent, where they may become suspicious of what's going on inside and even tempted to sabotage it, whether intentionally or not. Thus, a big tent approach sends a strong message, particularly to next-generation members and affines, about their potential value and contributions to the enterprise, and the importance of their involvement (Illustration 8).

But the approach requires careful, strategic orchestration.

Indeed, with an increasing number of families worldwide committed to family governance initiatives, they are in effect developing their own, idiosyncratic big tent approaches. Specifically, they are setting clear guidelines for how family members can engage meaningfully with, and contribute to, the family and its ever more complex and challenging business activities.

In lectures and presentations, when I share my observations of families who pursue the big tent approach, the metaphorical concept usually makes intuitive sense to listeners, no matter the country or audience type. But it's only when I describe what it feels like to be *left out* of the tent that the message really hits home.

The main example I share is when members of a founding generation explained to me that they wanted their legacy to be a family enterprise that survived across many generations. Immediately after, they stipulated that the wives of their two sons were to be excluded from all business conversations. In response, they were delicately reminded that the spouses were the mothers of their grandchildren, and therefore significant influences on how the third generation would see the business, and thus it may have made sense to "bring them into the tent"; they reconsidered and committed to establish meaningful non-operational roles for their daughters-in-law. Other, similar examples, such as those of affines who are excluded from "family" meetings, also tend to hit home.

Still, inclusion of family members for the sake of inclusion can be interpreted as a token gesture. The key, then, from my observations of insightful multigenerational family businesses, is to ensure that individuals are ready, willing, and capable to contribute in a meaningful way. I must emphasize the tripartite nature of this set of attributes, as implied by the use of the word "and" rather than "or." That is, the omission of any one of the three qualities—such as being ready and willing but not capable—means potential disaster, or at the very least a far from ideal situation for the family and enterprise. Readiness, willingness, and capability are mandatory qualities for contribution.

This discussion also raises the question of what it means to contribute to the enterprise. Again, observation of families who spend a considerable amount of time getting this right suggests that an ideal way to promote contribution is to design meaningful pathways to contribute. There's no one right set of such pathways, but there are many examples of these types of pathways:

- Executive
- Manager/supervisor
- Enterprise/entrepreneurship
- Family office
- Family governance
- Business governance
- Family philanthropy

Each of the pathway-related roles comes with a distinct set of requirements, responsibilities, and remuneration, all of which must be clearly articulated. See again my earlier caveat that all elements of the big tent approach require careful, strategic orchestration.

So how does it all come together?

Back inside the tent, when a family member who does not work in the business understands that there are meaningful ways that they can engage with the enterprise, such as through a family office or business governance role, they are more likely to feel valued. Likewise, a married-in will feel included when they hear about opportunities for involvement in the family's philanthropic activities. Or, when a rising-generation member finds out about the enterprise pathway, they will enthusiastically consider the family business a venture partner they may need in the future to execute their own entrepreneurial vision.

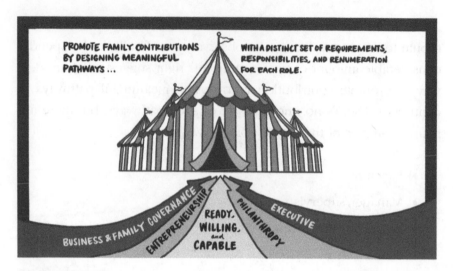

Illustration 8 THE BIG TENT APPROACH

Whatever the exact circumstance, the big tent approach helps the full range of family members to see new opportunities to contribute and to understand the need—and expectation—to have the required skill sets to deliver optimally in a given, appropriate role. That is, they recognize the importance of being ready, willing, and capable to contribute to the enterprise. This thinking is at the core of continuity modelling.

RIPCC Best Practice Dimensions

The RIPCC framework is something I have stolen, but paraphrased, from a book written by my friend and colleague Professor Emeritus John Ward. But given the remarkable number of books and articles John has produced to help readers understand family enterprises, it's difficult for me even to know from which work I got the idea!

Ward didn't call it the RIPCC framework, but as I recall, this is what he referred to when answering a question someone posed about what he believes families who get it right actually do, based on his decades of work with business families. I've paraphrased the lessons that these families have taught him into these five dimensions.

The first dimension, the one that begins with R, is that the families *respect* the challenge: that is, families who get it right understand that functioning optimally in a business-owning family is challenging. The second dimension, the I, reflects that Ward believes the *issues* across families are the same, but the perspectives are different. What that means, I suggest, is that the issues facing business-owning families are fundamentally the same, but how they manage and navigate these issues will vary, dependent on the perspectives of individuals and family groups. The third dimension relates to *planning*. Ward suggests that those who get it right don't leave it to chance. They are consummate planners. This dimension, though not intentionally framed as such, is at the epicenter of the Continuity Canvas and will be clear in Part II.

The fourth dimension of the RIPCC framework concerns *communication*. Ward suggests families who get it right are those who find ways to communicate. Finally, and arguably the most important of the RIPCC best practice framework dimensions, concerns having a *commitment*: to the "us" in question.

Taking those dimensions and contextualizing them for the *Continuity Model Generation*, it is simple to argue that continuity will be significantly enhanced if stakeholders understand five things: (i) respect that it will be challenging; (ii) understand that the issues may be the same across families but people will have different perspectives; (iii) recognize the importance of developing plans for ownership, family, and the many entities that are being managed; (iv) see communication as vital; and (v) believe that continuity won't occur without a commitment, a significant commitment, to what the family is trying to achieve. That's the RIPCC in action (Illustration 9).

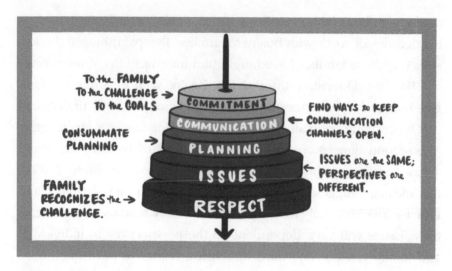

Illustration 9 RIPCC FRAMEWORK

Four Ps Framework

Related to the RIPCC framework, the four Ps framework is again una-bashedly stolen and paraphrased from Ward's work. And again, I can't direct you to exactly which publication it came from, but somewhere in those volumes is a section that relates to these four dimensions. From his experience observing and working with all types of business-owning families, Ward suggests there are four critical priorities, all of which start with "p." The first priority is *parenting*, and this is hard to argue against when you consider we are talking about families. The major contributors to the next generation, and this is really relevant for continuity modelling, are the parents, as reflected in the example I included in the earlier discussion of the big tent framework. Ward's recommendation here is that, to increase chances of harmony, optimal functioning, meaningful contributions, and other desirables, there needs to be a focus on being exemplary parents. The second "p" relates to familial *process*. My interpretation is that, too often, families get out of whack and forget to introduce ways to appreciate the fact that they are family. Most anyone involved in family business will agree that they are guilty of spending inordinate time talking about or being involved in the business, at the expense of their family. So, the second priority needs to be consciously and intentionally addressed by finding ways to include reminders that the family is a family. The third priority is one that receives immediate positive response whenever I share it: the imperative to put in place *protocols* before you need them. This refers especially to governance protocols and processes that set the expectations for now- and next-generation involvement, for example. The fourth priority is to develop a sense of *purpose* and understand the general and specific responsibilities of being part of a business-owning family (Illustration 10).

So, again, a lot of work and thinking has gone into understanding the priorities that a family should have. Parenting, familial processes, having protocols in place before they are needed, and developing a shared sense of purpose will individually and collectively contribute to addressing assumptions and be foundational in developing a continuity model mindset within the family.

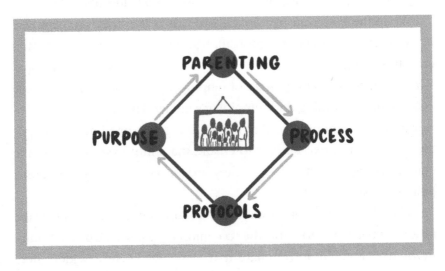

Illustration 10 THE FOUR Ps FRAMEWORK

Four Cs Framework

The fourth framework in the familial meta-framework is cut-and-pasted from the research of Professor Danny Miller and Professor Isabel LeBreton Miller. Their groundbreaking study of long-lived family-controlled businesses (FCBs) revealed that, unlike managers of most other for-profit businesses, those of FCBs seek ends in addition to profit. As such, they are more willing to make bold decisions (i.e. commands) that sacrifice some of their personal interests for the sake of their employees (i.e. community) and larger society (i.e. connections), as well as for the long-term survival of the businesses they operate (i.e. continuity).

According to the Millers, the *continuity* dimension is about having a focal mission and commitment to a set of related capabilities; *community* concerns having in place an appropriate internal employee base to formulate and implement the strategy; *connection* reflects that external stakeholders and resource–providers are crucial to being adaptive and being able to access scarce resources; *command* captures the context of governance and leadership (Illustration 11).

While the common perception of FCBs is that they are clannish, inward-thinking nests of nepotism, the exemplar firms in the Millers' study suggest otherwise. Their owning-families foster a cohesive organizational community of employees for whom joining these FCBs is akin to joining their employer's family. The families, then, are stewards who understand that the business is a precious asset and, therefore, go to great lengths to ensure that employees who join the community appreciate the role they are tasked to play in the family heirloom's sustainability.

The Millers position community as "uniting and tending to the tribe" (2005a, p. 38). For the community, association with family owners is far more intimate than it would be in a widely held firm. Millerian families appreciate that "to cherish the firm meant to treasure those who staff and sustain it" (2005b, p. 521). As members join a community in which adhering to deeply held values rooted in the founders' beliefs and institutionalized by subsequent generations is the principal driver—rather than bureaucratic rules or pecuniary incentives—selection processes are more comprehensive. Having a community of employees whose hearts and minds are engaged with the organization results in cohesive corporate cultures perpetuated through ongoing, intimate, trust-based relationships among community members and family owners. As a result, "stratospheric" levels of loyalty and motivation are characteristic of the cohesive internal community (2005b, p. 522). The Millers observe that building a "cohesive, gung-ho community of employees" (2005a, p. 38) contributes to a collectivist social philosophy in the outstanding FCBs in their study (e.g. the Hall family of the Hallmark Card Company). The elements of this tribal community include "strong values, not just stated, but pervasively enacted; incessant socialization in those values; a welfare state to enlist employees in the good fight; and an informal way of operating that engages interaction and collaboration" (2005a, p. 39).

Ultimately, the community of employees is charged with nurturing the "precious enterprise and strive to achieve its hallowed mission" (2005a, p. 42), by working with and on behalf of the family. They succeed together by displaying a "moral commitment to enter into an enduring relationship of broad reciprocity—like friendship or even kinship. . .a felt bond between employee and employer" (2005a, p. 42).

In addition to their close relationships with internal stakeholders, these FCBs are notorious for their embeddedness in their business networks. As such, they are more attuned to, cognizant of, and understanding of the need to navigate a slew of nuanced multidimensional challenges with respect to their business partners, challenges that their non-FCB contemporaries do not face. Connectivity to the broader society is considered particularly important due to an expectation and obligation to be especially generous to those that "treated them so well" (Miller and Le Breton-Miller 2005a, p. 44).

In contrast to community, the Millerian concept of connection is an externally oriented construct: "being good neighbors and partners" (2005a, p. 42). Just as concentrating on building enduring relationships with a community of employees is important, these FCBs seek similar mutually beneficial relationships with business partners, customers, and society. Being a "good neighbor and indispensable partner" (2005a, p. 42) is achieved by using "an ancient toolkit: being honest, farsighted, and generous" (2005a, p. 42). By being "meticulously honest" and delivering more than promised, "contacts grow into contracts, and contracts into age-old partnerships" (2005a, p. 43) (e.g. the Bechtel family). The Millers observe that successful FCBs favor "long-term, win-win relationships over transactions," and because they are driven by the will for the business to last, they are willing to "put time and money into potentially sustaining associations that take a long time to pay off" (2005a, p. 43). They are, moreover, characterized as benevolent partners who build a "devoted cadre of supply chain soul mates" (2005a, p. 44). By being more responsive and committed, they form close bonds with customers and maintain them over time, often adopting a philosophy that "there is no such thing as an ex-customer" (2005a, p. 44).

In sum, the focus on prioritizing commitment both to building a community of employees passionate about adherence to the family's values-driven culture and to developing long-term, trust-based connections with loyal partners results in heightened levels of intimacy, which enables family business managers to share the feelings of and better understand their employees and business partners. In this way, families often "absorb misery" (Miller and Le Breton-Miller, 2005a, p. 40) when stakeholders face challenging situations. Consider the following events recalled by Walter Haas Jr., then-Chairman of the board of Levi Straus, in 1973 when faced with a stock-price plummet from $59.75 to $16.62:

> *"It was one of the worst six months of my life, very bad, not so much for the monetary loss, but for the pride. It was a reflection on our management. A big part of it was that so many little people were let down. We were terribly distressed about the stock because we had made a point of setting aside shares for our own employees when we went public. They were unsophisticated investors, and this debacle, coupled with the huge drop in the market in general."* Haas's voice faltered, the disappointment still keen, five years later.
>
> *(Cray 1978, p. 218).*

The Millers define command as leaders, both those within the family and throughout the top management team, "acting independently and adapting freely" (2005a, p. 45). Their outstanding families view the freedom to act decisively and courageously as a vital source of their "competitive originality and business renewal" (2005a, p. 45). A common theme among these leaders is the ability to embrace unorthodoxy and break the rules. This ability is fortified when managers believe in one another and act for the company without the burden of worrying about termination. Yet, it is important to note that due to the managers' responsibility for the long-run viability of the business and the reputation of the family, "boldness takes form not in gambles, but in programs of courageous, targeted adaption" (2005a, p. 48). In other words, although leaders exercising command must have "the clout, expertise, and motivation to act courageously," those decisions must also be "in the interest of the company" (2005b, p. 525).

The knowledge of the perspectives of employees and business partners gained through intimate associations with these stakeholders provides family business leaders a platform from which they can assess how to behave with unusual boldness without disenfranchising those with whom they have created a unity of purpose. Consider the following situation and exchange involving Corning Glass Ware's non-family CEO Tom MacAvoy and family owner and Chairman Amory Houghton in 1979:

> *When faced with a major issue with a product line, MacAvoy remembers listening to legal advice to gather more facts and proceed deliberately before he and Houghton decided to act on the basis of simple criteria. "It gradually became apparent that our reputation, our integrity, was being questioned by some of our key people", said MacAvoy, who found that intolerable. "If you have a dozen people who disbelieve that the company means what it says about quality and dealing with customers, its [sic] poison. So I remember I went next door and knocked on Amo's door, which happened to be closed. I opened the door, and he was there with his secretary. I said, "I've just decided we are going to recall the Corning Ware Electromatic Coffee pots." He was dictating a letter or something like that. He said, "How much is it going to cost?" I said, "I don't know, but it's probably going to be 10 million dollars or something like that". So, he nodded his head, and I went back and did it. It cost $14 million, but it was the right thing to do.*
>
> *(Dyer and Gross 2001, p. 348).*

As this example shows, the ability to sense employees' and customers' failing confidence in the business was the impetus for action. In the absence of a continuity mindset, MacAvoy might not have been mindful of the impact the company's product line was having on its community and connections. Yet, his awareness of their feelings toward Corning and, more importantly, the importance to Corning of maintaining intimate relationships with them, provided the rationale he needed to spearhead what ultimately became a $14-million recall, a considerable expense (especially in 1979 dollars).

In sum, families that exercise command empower their leaders to make bold decisions that, while not always in the short-term economic interest of the FCB, support its social relationships with employees and business partners.

In the Millers' successful FCBs, the commitment to continuity through a clear intention to keep the business within the family is evident. These companies express a desire for long-term survival of the business, which results from "the relentless development of the capabilities needed to realize it" (2005a, p. 35). Continuity for these families, their companies, and the leaders at the helm in each generation means being united in their laser focus on continuing to do something better than anyone else and an understanding that achievement of this objective requires the patient investment of both financial and human resources.

In sum, the higher purpose of FCBs is to provide for future generations' fulfillment, not only economically but socially. The essence of continuity, therefore, is devotion to a greater cause, which encompasses

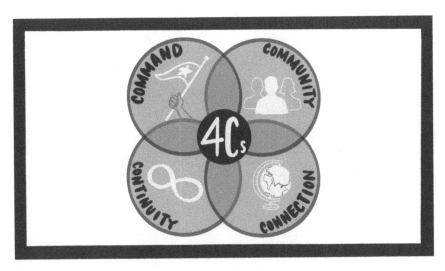

Illustration 11 THE FOUR Cs FRAMEWORK

Familial Meta-Framework

social and economic objectives (Tomer 2001). Thus, the contention is that family business manager–stewards who have the capacity to be courageous decision-makers and are able to strike the delicate balance between their self- and other-regarding interests will increase their chances of continuity.

Individual Meta-Framework

The sixteen dimensions that make up the four frameworks of the Individual meta-framework consider the gamut of questions everyone must answer at some point on their life journey. Most, if not all, relate to roles removed from those in the family business; such is their richness.

Five Servant Leadership Dimensions

Continuity, by its very nature, requires servant leaders. Barbuto and Wheeler's (2006) servant leader dimensions of wisdom, empathy, altruism, persuasiveness, and stewardship reflect hallmark attributes and behaviors of the continuity model generation (Illustration 12).

Wisdom can be understood as a combination of awareness of surroundings and anticipation of consequences. When leaders have both characteristics, they are adept at picking up cues from the environment and understanding their implications. Indeed, leaders high in wisdom are characteristically observant and anticipatory across most functions and settings (Bierly et al. 2000). Wisdom is the ideal union of perfect and practical, combining the height of knowledge and utility.

Emotional healing (empathy) describes a leader's commitment to and skill in fostering spiritual recovery from hardship or trauma. Leaders who are highly empathetic and great listeners are adept at facilitating the healing process. In organizations, such leaders create environments that are safe for employees to voice personal and professional issues. Followers who experience personal traumas will also turn to leaders high in emotional healing.

Altruistic calling (altruism) describes a leader's deep-rooted desire to make a positive difference in others' lives. It is a generosity of the spirit consistent with a philanthropic purpose in life. Because the ultimate goal is to serve, leaders high in altruistic calling will put others' interests ahead of their own and will diligently work to meet followers' needs.

Persuasive mapping (persuasiveness) describes the extent to which leaders use sound reasoning and mental frameworks. Leaders high in persuasive mapping are skilled at mapping issues and conceptualizing greater possibilities and are compelling when articulating these opportunities. They encourage others to visualize the organization's future, and motivate others to do things, without being coercive or manipulative.

Organizational stewardship describes the extent to which leaders prepare an organization to make a positive contribution to society through community development, programs, and outreach. Such stewardship involves an ethic or value related to taking responsibility for the wellbeing of the community and making sure that the strategies and decisions undertaken reflect the commitment to give back and leave things better than found. Stewards also work to develop a community spirit in the workplace, laying the groundwork for leaving a positive legacy.

The concept of servant leadership has long been fundamental for the third generation Nelson family, and their global company, Kemin Industries. It is what drives their culture and their shared philosophy of management and leadership. To signal the importance of servant leadership in their organizational fiber, the family leadership team commissioned me to conduct a study in 2018 to further define servant leadership and establish, then monitor, how it mattered to their company. In other words, while the concept of servant leadership was firmly embedded in the organization, given the evolution to a future-focused global company, and being a science-based organization, the leaders thought it time to put some science (i.e. theory-based, empirical evidence) behind their philosophical approach to commerce.

The research team first confirmed that, according to the academic literature and extant studies, servant leaders focus on building a loving and caring community, generating a shared vision for helping others, and creating the freedom and resources for employees to become servants themselves, as their primary motivation is to serve others (Greenleaf 1977). Also, aligned with Greenleaf's (1977) warning that servant leadership would be difficult to operationalize, they learned that theoretical development of this construct had been slow partially because it is more than just a management technique but a way of life that begins with "the natural feeling that one wants to serve, to serve first" (Greenleaf 1977, p. 7). It was further confirmed that servant leadership is a multidimensional construct where the leader places the good of those being led over their own self-interest, emphasizes employee development, displays stewardship of organizational resources, builds community, and practices empathy, humility, and authenticity. Confirming the 'Kemin Way', servant leadership requires social exchanges that are long term, enduring, and ongoing, where individuals maintain consistency and fairness. Importantly, and very relevant to the Nelson family, the review of the servant leadership literature highlighted that by building a loving and caring community, servant leaders create a multigenerational legacy of serving others first. To refine our understanding and application of servant leadership, we utilized Barbuto and Wheeler's (2006) Servant Leadership Questionnaire (SLQ).

Organizational stewardship was most aligned with continuity and is defined as committing first and foremost to serving other's needs. Servant leaders recognize the role of organizations is to create people who will build a better tomorrow, and therefore, they build "people first" organizations that emphasize service. Organizational stewardship assumes responsibility for the wellbeing of others and ensures organizational strategies and decisions to make a positive difference. Servant-led organizations act as caretakers and role models working for the common interest of society, developing a community spirit in the workspace, and building a positive legacy. As Greenleaf (1977, p. 60) said, "the only way to change a society is to produce people, enough people, who will change it."

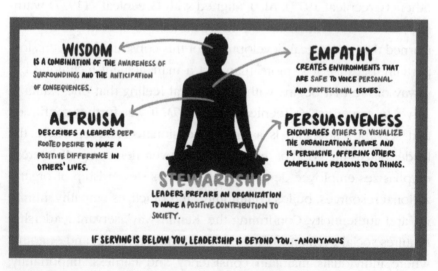

WISDOM
IS A COMBINATION OF THE AWARENESS OF SURROUNDINGS AND THE ANTICIPATION OF CONSEQUENCES.

EMPATHY
CREATES ENVIRONMENTS THAT ARE SAFE TO VOICE PERSONAL AND PROFESSIONAL ISSUES.

ALTRUISM
DESCRIBES A LEADER'S DEEP ROOTED DESIRE TO MAKE A POSITIVE DIFFERENCE IN OTHERS' LIVES.

PERSUASIVENESS
ENCOURAGES OTHERS TO VISUALIZE THE ORGANIZATION'S FUTURE AND IS PERSUASIVE, OFFERING OTHERS COMPELLING REASONS TO DO THINGS.

STEWARDSHIP
LEADERS PREPARE AN ORGANIZATION TO MAKE A POSITIVE CONTRIBUTION TO SOCIETY.

IF SERVING IS BELOW YOU, LEADERSHIP IS BEYOND YOU. -ANONYMOUS

Illustration 12 SERVANT LEADERSHIP FRAMEWORK

To servant leaders, organizations play a moral role in society to give back and make things better than when they found them.

Four Tests Framework

The four tests framework is borrowed and paraphrased from arguably my favorite family enterprise article, which was authored by pioneering scholar-consultant, and Kellogg School of Management colleague, Professor Ivan Lansberg and published in the *Harvard Business Review*. The paper is well worth reading, then rereading. In fact, I advise anyone involved in business-owning families to become familiar with the paper, not necessarily with its intimate details, but at least with the broad concepts.

Like many of the frameworks included in the 21, it is possible to take a "napkin" perspective of the 4 tests. In the article, titled "The Four Tests of a Prince," Lansberg shares that there are four tests or hurdles that individuals will need to pass, not just once but across their tenure of involvement with the family enterprise. This is true regardless of whether involvement is to be in an operational or governance role in the business or family, or as a contributor in any other capacity.

The four tests, specifically, are the qualifying test, the self-imposed test, the circumstantial test, and the political test (Illustration 13). First, the qualifying test. I use a simple question to paraphrase Lansberg's idea for this one: When reviewing an individual for a position or role, would an independent, objective evaluator agree that this person is qualified? For a typical (not family enterprise) interview process, it is likely that multiple people will have the same or equal qualifications, with impressive CVs and other supporting material. Only those most qualified will make the final cut, so being qualified is necessary but not sufficient; the independent, objective evaluator will look for other indications to make a decision. These indications can be discovered through the other three tests.

For the self-imposed test, the question is whether an independent, objective evaluator would see enough evidence that the candidate has imposed upon themselves sufficient discipline to address any shortcomings in their qualifications. An example could be that although an individual is well-qualified in terms of their academic pedigree, they have pursued industry involvement or pro bono work above and beyond that which is required of them in their previous roles. Or it might be that the person's undergraduate degree at a certain institution had a focus on marketing and, knowing that any future senior role in their field required advanced qualifications in finance or governance, they have complemented their undergraduate training with a master's focused on these areas: or the other way around, where they supplemented a finance degree with graduate work in marketing. So, while self-imposed tests are open to interpretation, an independent objective evaluator will generally be looking for something above the stated qualifications for the position. For the self-imposed test you could also include what work the person has undertaken to contribute to the development, implementation, or functioning of family governance roles, which are typically voluntary. Of course, like many of the 21 frameworks, the conversation this test requires is equally applicable to non-family business conversations.

The third of the four tests, the circumstantial test, involves behaviors that indicate, objectively, how the candidate has responded in situations that do not reflect "business as usual." For example, someone might have volunteered to close down a non-performing division. So, this person ran toward the fire to put it out, rather than hiding and leaving difficult decisions and communications to someone else. The current COVID-19 pandemic offers a great context for such examples, as crises provide inspiring leaders the best chance to show their true strengths and potential. The independent objective evaluator understands that at some point the candidate's mettle will be tested by a crisis and having exposure to these unpredictable

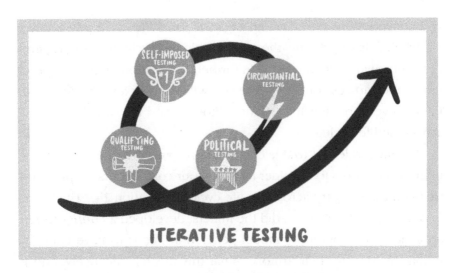

Illustration 13 THE FOUR TESTS FRAMEWORK

circumstances will hone their leadership and/or governance skills, or their preparedness to lead or govern.

The fourth test is the political test, which does not refer to politics. Rather, it is about the ability or capacity of the individual to navigate the often-turbulent political environment brought about by the utility heterogeneity in the ownership system, the diversity in expectations, engagement and skill levels of a growing family group, and the multiple agendas involved in managing the increasingly diverse portfolio of commercial activities. These three systems, combined, give rise to a potentially politically charged workplace, family place, and ownership place that requires a certain capacity and tolerance.

Being cognizant of these four individual meta-framework tests will help to develop a continuity model mindset.

Four Leadership Priorities

The leadership literature is massive. The most practical and applicable approach for continuity modelers uses the leadership concepts and conversations based on an organizational life cycle perspective. Dr. Ichak Adizes presents the most usable life cycle perspective, and I encourage anyone interested in further information on this to spend time on the adizes.com site. Here you will discover a very interactive, informative approach that includes normal and abnormal problems across the life cycle.

But most relevant to this conversation—and the stickiest concept in this domain—is to consider how the four core leadership priorities (defined below) vary across the life cycle (Illustration 14). The benefit of this is that Adizes, as did the Millers, developed a *configuration* approach. The continuity model generation needs to have configuration thinking in their armory. What this means, effectively, and it applies to many of the concepts introduced in these pages, is that the dimensions are all evident, but how they should be configured will vary. Examples of how this manifests into multiple configurations of a Continuity Canvas will be covered in Part III.

Now let's apply that thinking to Adizes's four leadership priorities. The four priorities are production, administration, integration, and entrepreneurship. The idea is that first there is a need to *produce* something. As a leader you have to focus on that initially, and at some point in the life cycle of the organization, *administration* becomes a priority. This eventually becomes unsustainable without *integration* across the various functions, once an entity reaches a certain level of maturity. And finally, without *entrepreneurship* there will be no chance of reinvention and innovation to change and adapt to the shifting environment.

So, a leader has to do two things. First, they have to understand that these functions (production, administration, integration, and entrepreneurship) should be their major foci. Then they need to understand how to configure them differently, depending on the life cycle of their organization. In the early stages of the business, for example, their focus will be on production and entrepreneurship. As the business venture evolves, they will continue to emphasize those priorities, but also administration. As things evolve even more, the

46

focus on production may attenuate because that's in place already, but integration becomes a greater priority.

The most effective way to capture this changing configuration is to use either a capital or lowercase letter for each priority. The aim of the game, according to Adizes, is to get in the prime life cycle stage and stay in it. In the prime stage, the P (production), A (administration), I (integration), and E (entrepreneurship) are all in focus; they are joint priorities. Leading up to that point, they will be in different configurations. As I mentioned earlier, beyond the prime stage, in a mature organization, you'll find that entrepreneurship fades; it's important to be cognizant of this.

The *Continuity Model Generation* understands that looking through a life cycle lens reveals so much about the business's overall health. They will ensure as part of their mantra and their guiding principles, that the aim of the game is to get in prime and stay in prime, the life cycle stage where all four priorities of leadership are in concurrent focus. They are aware of the tendency in mature organizations for administration to rule the conversation, and to lose—or not prioritize—entrepreneurship and strategic risk-taking. Another mantra or guiding

Illustration 14 FOUR LEADERSHIP PRIORITIES

47

Individual Meta-Framework

principle for leaders in emerging businesses or entities is to understand that their job is to prepare the organization for the next stage of the life cycle as it approaches nirvana, which is prime. Or, alternatively, to understand if they have moved from prime to maturity, how to move back to prime, the stage that can be depicted simply as P, A, I, E.

Four Exit Strategies

Exiting significant, long-term career roles is difficult. Those who study this phenomenon, not necessarily in the family business context, have established that there are four exit strategies. Like the other 20 frameworks, the one for exits presents an efficient, effective way of understanding a potentially problematic topic for continuity modelers.

Here are the four established, role-based strategies to transition from a significant role in the business or family: ambassador, governor, general, and monarch (Illustration 15). Understanding these four exit strategies is useful. The preferred strategies are to depart as an ambassador or governor. Like many of the concepts and labels in the 21 framework dimensions, these are self-explanatory. An ambassador moves from an operational role to an ambassadorial role. The best example I have seen of this was when a CEO anointed his son to take over the business, and his announcement came with a message that he would still be involved in the business in an ambassador role. What this meant, and how it manifested, was that he was appointed by the board to promote and represent the business at specific events, as appropriate. The benefits of this are obvious. The message is clear, and it is recommended that some version of this is at least discussed with those leaving significant long-tenure leadership roles in operating businesses. But the idea is also relevant to board and family roles.

The second exit strategy is the governor. Here, the individual would move from an operational role to a governance role, as appropriate. This would ensure that their network continues to add value to the business, and provide a way for their institutional memory, typically substantial, to inform the next generation in their quest to continue differently. This governor role could be either in the family or in the business, as a full-time, paid non-executive director or in some meaningful advisory capacity. Again, it is worth the discussion to ensure individuals exit into a meaningful role and are able to continue to contribute.

The third exit strategy is known as the general. This strategy, which is non-optimal, occurs more often than it should. The idea is that the individual exits their role but plots their return, ready to make their move at the first sign of crisis, big or small. As soon as any cracks appear in their successor's way of handling the business or related activities, the general is ready to step in, typically with the mindset that the business cannot operate without them: just as a military commander would suggest that their troop or battalion wouldn't be as effective under someone else's lead. Again, this exit strategy is worthy of discussion and even to call out to a longtime leader who may be tempted to pursue it. Also, it can be wise to have directors put into place protocols, guidelines, and/or policies to ensure that a leader aspiring to general is directed into a governing or ambassadorial role, to minimize the chance of their reappearance.

The fourth exit strategy is not so much an exit strategy as a leadership right. That's because the monarch doesn't actually exit. They stay on the throne, typically, until they die or are overthrown. End of story (and the beginning of a new one).

Exit strategies, once identified, can be either formalized or guarded against. I recommend the formalizing of roles as either ambassadors and/or governors and guarding against the potential for leaving with all the pomp and ceremony of a military general, only to have the "departed" leader reappear in full battle fatigues in the not-so-distant future. And obviously if a monarch is in place, and sometimes that is appropriate, you must understand that there will be a time, potentially a sudden one, when there will be a transition to a new leader and to spend the time putting in place, formally or informally, structures and processes to ensure a smooth transition.

Individual Meta-Framework

One thing we do know is that when matriarchs of families pass, there is a period of considerable flux. Some families have waited patiently while their mother or grandmother are still alive and have not been transparent about their discord-sowing intentions, so as to not upset this important family figure. But once she has passed, the glue that forms the bond and holds the family together dissolves. It's like when the gloves come off in a fight, catalyzing a bitter, often ongoing, often costly conflict. Understanding the probability that this will happen is a good starting point. Countering it in advance is highly recommended.

The four exit strategies speak for themselves in the context of continuity. For instance, if there is a monarchy in place and that leader will rule until they die, there needs to be a way to ensure that their ultimate demise does not negatively impact chances of continuity, as noted above. In general, continuity model generation members are conscious of the four exit strategies, and typically would guard against the generals and monarchs, and facilitate doing what it takes to make sure that governors and ambassadors are able to contribute meaningfully beyond their operational roles.

Illustration 15 FOUR EXIT STRATEGIES FRAMEWORK

Generational Meta-Framework

The *Continuity Model Generation* is future-focused, by definition. Consideration of the 12 dimensions of the generational meta-framework forces reflection on the circumstances that surround now and next generations. A central theme of this meta-framework is the understanding that what got you here won't get you where you want and need to be.

Four Ls Framework

If there's a standout framework in the 21 frameworks in this book, it would be the 4 Ls. This approach, first introduced by Professor Emeritus Ken Moores and Professor Mary Barrett, has been a mainstay of every family enterprise education program I have delivered in the past two decades. Students and participants in these programs, no matter their age, education, culture, or experience, have responded more to this framework than any other. As such, it has also driven the framework approach shared in this book. Like many of the other frameworks, because it is simple and easy to draw, the four Ls framework is easy to digest and share. Importantly, it is theory-driven and evidence-based. The research on which the framework is based is 280 pages long. The chapter on it in a previous book, written by Moores and me (Craig and Moores 2017), is 30 pages long. But, for the sake of this book's approach, I'll share the main components of the framework in a few hundred words. Here goes.

Two theoretical perspectives drive the four Ls framework: the life cycle of the individual and learning theory. But you don't need to know much about those. What you need to know is that it is inevitable that you will transition through the four Ls or learning stages. Most everyone reading this does. Specifically, you will first learn business; second, learn your family business; third, learn to lead your family business; and fourth, you will need to learn to let go (Illustration 16).

There's more to this framework than I think even Moores and Barrett initially expected when they undertook the study in question and wrote their book (Moores and Barrett 2003). One reason for this is that in its original form, the four Ls framework relates to an audience working in the business. While some in the Continuity Generation Modeling conversation will be working in the business, many won't be. They will have other roles, predominantly those related to governance. But even if they're not in operational roles, they need to learn business. Likewise, it is necessary for them to learn the family business and learn to lead, but that leadership will be in a governing role, in their case. And learning to let go of that governance position is equally important.

The four Ls framework, moreover, serves as a human resource tracking tool. It is fundamentally a talent development map. Anyone in the family enterprise ecosystem needs to appreciate that as they evolve across their life cycle, they will require increasingly deeper understanding of the intricacies of the family, business, and ownership systems: specifically, to understand the values that drive decision-making.

In the interest of space, the two quadrants we will focus on here are L2, learning the family business, and L4, learning to let go. Let's start with the fourth L, which is actually the most difficult. That bears repeating: learning to let go is the most difficult of all learning components in family enterprise. The reason for that is the emotional attachment anyone who has had a long-term tenure or association with a business will have. To let go will be a challenge and will link closely to the four exit stages introduced earlier in the book.

Everyone will inevitably need to address the reality of letting go. Having a plan is important. Sticking to the plan is challenging. The recommendation is to find someone who 'got it right' and learn from them. I wish I had a dollar for every time I have been told, "I will never retire." And there is no need to retire. Just repurpose. Transition from one set of activities to another in a planned manner. Move from being available to the business seven days a week, 365 days a year to something less than that. Then after that is comfortable, less still. Replace the "work" responsibilities with "other." The people who get it right report that "I have never been busier since I 'retired."

The second L, while perhaps not as difficult as the fourth, is the most important of the four. In the second L, it is important to learn the "value of values," to keep the philosophies of the incumbent and previous generations, but not the exact detail, in order to continue differently. Anyone serious about continuity model generation participation will need to know that previous line by heart and be prepared to repeat it verbatim to anyone, anywhere, anytime. In the second L, it's important that individuals in operating roles have profit responsibility if they intend to move into leadership roles within the business or its governance. It is also in this quadrant that individuals need to address impostor syndrome. It is here that they need to spend ample time building their own individual brand. It is here that they must gain the respect of others. It is here that they need to make sure that they have the trust of others, too, as they move into more senior operation or governance roles.

Thus, understanding the importance of this second L is crucial. It serves as a foundation for the development of the successor's talent development plan within the Continuity Canvas, as we'll discuss.

Individuals and families who get this right populate the simple four-quadrant L diagram to understand their situation now and what it would look like in five or ten years. Most people want to rush into the third quadrant ("learn to lead the family business"), a temptation fraught with danger. Leadership is tough. Whether in a governance or operational role, leaders need to make hard decisions; if they parachute into this role prematurely, they will be set up for failure. I recommend spending as much time as possible in the second L, to genuinely understand what distinguishes the family.

This distinction, further, is typically based on the values and beliefs of the founder, as interpreted by the second generation and ultimately institutionalized, but which require full understanding and revisiting. Moreover, as noted earlier, it's critical to understand the importance of keeping previous generations' philosophies that are part of the organization's DNA, but not the detail. Rising leaders will face many technical, environmental, demographic, and societal changes as they pursue an ambitious program to continue differently; but in the second L they will have cover of the incumbent generation. This means that they can bring about change *incrementally* rather than radically. They can ask questions without fear or favor. They can consider things that they can change prior to moving into more senior roles, whether these be organizational, structural, personnel, or strategic modifications, such as ensuring that, as future leaders, they have the ideal personnel in place on their executive team, the people they want most as board directors, and the support of valued, trusted advisors. Also, legal entities can be revised and made appropriate for what is needed on their watch, and for subsequent generations. These conversations need to happen while they are in the second L, where there is space for robust debate. They can afford the time to be patient while the incumbent generation prepares and learns to let go.

Critically, as the next generation transitions to senior leadership, they can co-lead. Co-leading with the incumbent generation will bring comfort to the many stakeholders earnestly watching this

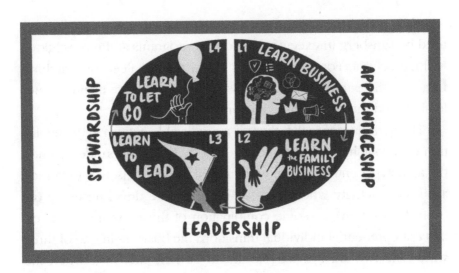

Illustration 16 THE FOUR Ls FRAMEWORK

process. Ask any financier and they will tell you that the thing that keeps them up at night is the next-generation-leadership decision. Any major supplier will tell you that they are comfortable with the current arrangement with the long-term decision-maker in place, as they know that this situation won't jeopardize their relationship. Any customer will tell you the same thing. Any long-term employee, exactly the same. The fundamental question that all stakeholders want answered is "Are we in good hands?" This relates to family as much as it does to the business context.

There are 21 frameworks that make up the 6 meta-frameworks in this book. As suggested earlier, the four Ls framework is among the most important and, like the others, the simplicity of it masks the complexity. It is a crucial element of the *Continuity Model Generation*.

Four Ownership Stages

Scholars and practitioners have introduced many variations of the four ownership stages framework over the past three decades. The one that makes the most sense and is easiest to share is a version used by Lansberg in executive education programs at the prestigious Kellogg School. For several years I had the privilege of watching Lansberg share this approach in his teaching and have again shamelessly tested this on multiple audiences worldwide.

The genesis idea is that there is a predictable pattern in the evolution of ownership. It begins for everybody with the founder–owner, the archetypal entrepreneur, who takes it upon themselves to launch a business activity whether based on an innate drive, necessity (or even desperation), or some combination of those. As time evolves, that entrepreneurial individual transitions the business in one of three ways. The two ways most relevant to us here are, first, when the founder transitions to a single-successor business, a model dominant in countries such as Japan. In this case, a specific individual, usually the first-born, is anointed to continue the business as a single owner. The second, more popular option is that the business or assets are transferred or transitioned to a sibling partnership. The third option for the owner is a liquidity event via a public offering or management buyout. This third scenario is not relevant to this conversation but suffice it to say that when the business is sold, a problem is replaced by another problem!

In sum, then, most businesses at one point adopted a founding–owner structure, and that founder eventually, during their life cycle, transitioned ownership to either a single owner–successor offspring or a partnership made up of their children, or a sibling partnership (Illustration 17).

Lansberg goes to great lengths to stress that a founding owner is not equipped to do what a sibling partnership needs to do, though the founder often thinks they can. A founder and classic entrepreneur, in short, does not play well with others. They are the king or queen of their domain, typically ruling by stealth and influencing by virtue of their position as the major shareholder and creator of their entity. This situation will change for the successor–sibling generation, who will need to take a team-based rather than individual approach, as they are obligated to work with their siblings in joint ownership roles. This radical shift facilitates changes in structure and systems, and often involves changing strategy as well as, obviously, people. Moving from the first-generation owner to second-generation sibling ownership requires change, often of the radical sort, because the second generation is not able to operate in the same manner as the first generation.

If the founder–owner moves the ownership to a single successor, it is more likely that incremental change will occur, because in this case the focus will generally be on a change of personnel only. In this scenario, the second-generation single successor is taking over leadership of something that will probably mimic that which was in place, particularly in the short term, and definitely while the founding owner still has some influence and control over their anointed successor.

Moving back to the sibling partnership, here the structures have changed, and the systems have changed because the owners have changed. So, governing a sibling partnership requires a whole suite of different forums that were not needed when the single founder-owner was in charge. Sibling partnerships are difficult because each of the individuals involved brings a different skill set and mindset and, often, different expectations. Consider the earlier keystone framework that described in more granularity the ownership circle of the three circles model, noting that some will be there for economic reasons, or a dividend, while others will be there for psychological or emotional priorities centered around their attachment to, in this case, their father or mother. This is not right or wrong, but just the way it is in any heterogeneous group. So, forums need to be changed.

Consider also that the issues will be the same but that individual perspectives are different (as suggested by our discussion of the RIPCC framework earlier in the book).

At this point in the conversation, it becomes evident that the frameworks introduced in these pages have deep messages that apply across the entire 21 frameworks in our 6 meta-frameworks. They are not exclusive; indeed, they are often mutually *inclusive* and, when integrated, can assist in explaining or supporting other frameworks throughout this section of the book.

Moving from a sibling partnership, in which the offspring of the founder—who have typically been socialized in one house, under one roof—to a cousin consortium is again a radical change. Just as founders aren't equipped to function as sibling partners would, sibling partners as owners do not typically have what it takes to function in a cousin consortium ownership structure. So, this second radical change, this second paradigm shift, requires a focus, yet again, on new structures, new strategies, and new systems because it involves new people. Moreover, this extended team populated by a group of cousins who have been socialized within different families is much more complex and challenging than the previous ownership structures.

However, there is hope, because if the second generation has the presence of mind to understand that what got them to where they are will not be adequate, in structural terms, to get them to continue, and have already worked diligently on governance structures in the family and the business to establish appropriate forums that will facilitate clarity related to expectations and harmony related to business activities and returns, then they will recognize that incremental change will now be required. Indeed, the structures, systems, and processes that the second and third generation typically introduce will likely require only ongoing incremental innovation. Simplistically, if everything is in place, all that you need to do is change the people. The focus will be to prepare the people for the roles that the sibling partnership and/or the first cadre of the cousin consortium has introduced.

When Lansberg teaches this approach, he uses a sports analogy. He describes a founder–owner as a singles tennis player who, with support of a team of professionals, arrives on the court with a laser focus to win. The sibling partnership, he suggests, is more like a soccer or basketball team, in which there are multiple individuals who are collectively focused and bring different skill sets through their positional priorities on the field, but who are determined to succeed by winning the game as a team. The cousin consortium in this analogy is equivalent to a basketball organization or soccer club, in which there are multiple levels of teams: there is a significant administration role and significant managerial oversight, as well as on-field positions.

This sports analogy makes evident that a singles tennis player is not well-equipped to play in a multiple-member team event with others with complementary skills. Moreover, that person is rarely equipped to move into an administration role that would be required in a soccer club with many more moving parts for which they are ultimately responsible but cannot influence the same way that they influenced their single team activity. Similarly, a basketball team member, akin to a sibling partnership team, arguably does not hold the appropriate skill sets to work in a larger organization where they would have limited influence over non-athletic processes.

For continuity model generation members, understanding this evolution is crucial because they are likely at some point to need to understand that continuity modeling is very much about what is required in a cousin consortium stage. If they are currently in a second-generation situation there needs to be a shift, a radical change in structures, systems, and strategy, to enhance the likelihood of continuing past the third generation.

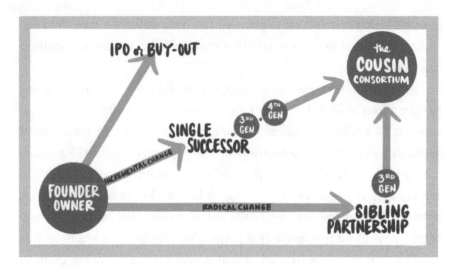

Illustration 17 FOUR OWNERSHIP STAGES

Four Entrepreneurship Principles

I borrowed and paraphrased the four entrepreneurship principles framework from work by Professor Saras Sarasvathy under the umbrella term "effectual reasoning." YouTube™ it; it's interesting. The thesis is that the entrepreneurial process is divided into five dimensions. For our purposes, we can safely jettison the framework's fifth dimension: the pilot in the plane. Sarasvathy suggests that entrepreneurs can be depicted by activities described as (i) the bird in the hand, (ii) affordable loss, (iii) the crazy quilt, and (iv) the lemonade principle. Part of the appeal of this approach is that the seemingly simple, catchy labels are rich with texture and, importantly, theory-driven and derived from evidence collected for Sarasvathy's seminal PhD work. Moreover, each can be linked to the four foundation theories included in the keystone meta-framework, as yet another example of how the concepts in the 21 frameworks can be integrated or collapsed to support one another.

Let's consider each of the four entrepreneurship principles. The bird in the hand relates directly to resources. The argument is that entrepreneurs understand and can harness the power of the resources most closely available to them. Dominant among these is an understanding of who they are, what they know, and who they know. These resources are easily accessible, thus the analogy of the bird in the hand, versus the bird in the bush. This approach is easy to extend and apply to family enterprises. Families in business understand and can leverage who they are, what they know, and whom they know, to contribute significantly to continuity.

The second principle is about affordable loss. Entrepreneurs, according to effectual reasoning, do not waste energy focusing on how much they're going to make; instead, they focus on how much they can afford to lose. Again, as family enterprises evolve over time there is a need to take risks, managed risks. Understanding the need to establish an approach based on affordable loss will keep the business relevant and potentially set the foundation for transformation or reinvention.

The third principle, the crazy quilt, suggests that likeminded individuals come together with different resources and skill sets to do something meaningful, practical, and useful. The Millers' (first introduced in the four C framework) way to describe this is that families in business pursue a substantive mission by doing something important exceedingly well. Sarasvathy's version draws on an understanding of quilting groups and communities as made up of people who come together to create something (a quilt) that is colorful, unique, and distinctive, but also of practical use in that it keeps you warm. So, for families in multigenerational businesses focused on continuity, again integrating one of the other frameworks, specifically the big tent, I suggest that the community is members of the family or families coming together with significant diversity and heterogeneity but committed to a shared vision. The shared vision, of course, is continuity. Thus, we can suggest that family members have come together to produce a "continuity quilt."

The fourth principle is the lemonade principle. This simply suggests the necessity to pivot. Entrepreneurs need to understand that if you come across lemons, you make lemonade, as the saying goes. What is required for continuity modelers, then, is the skill to be flexible, adaptable, and malleable because situations will and do change.

Taken collectively, the four principles have wide-ranging application to the continuity model generation. They must see themselves as entrepreneurs who understand the need to harness the resources at their disposal and not become preoccupied with how much they individually are going to make rather than how much they collectively can afford to lose; on behalf of the extended stakeholder group they get together with likeminded, albeit diverse, others to produce something meaningful and to achieve something meaningful, in this case social as well as economic performance; and they need to understand that situations will and do change (Illustration 18).

The four entrepreneurship principles offer a comparatively easy story to tell, placing the related concepts very much in line with the broad approach of this book: to harness the value of frameworks and meta-frameworks to understand and implement continuity differently.

Illustration 18 FOUR ENTREPRENEURSHIP PRINCIPLES

Tactical Meta-Framework

Being tactically savvy requires a clear understanding of how and why you are where you are, as well as who and what are going to get the family, the business, and the owners across upcoming chasms. The tactical meta-framework considers all of this. . .and more.

Family Enterprise Heterogeneity Frameworks

The family enterprise heterogeneity framework is actually the focus of a previous book I wrote with Professor Emeritus Ken Moores, *Leading a Family Business: Best Practices for Long-term Stewardship*. The framework is divided into two sections. The first is an organizational level and looks at that which distinguishes family businesses from other businesses in terms of their architecture, governance, entrepreneurship, and stewardship. The second section takes an individual level of analysis and describes the individual as a steward, an architect, a governor, and an entrepreneur (Illustration 19).

Let's summarize the components of the organizational level. Architecture, in this case, refers to the structures and systems in place to deliver the agreed-upon strategy. The core message here is that there is no point in developing a strategy unless it is consistent with the ability to implement that strategy through the appropriate structures and systems. Structures frame the organizational design, supporting the processes needed to create order and to carry out organizational tasks. Structures dictate (i) organizational activities, and (ii) the authority and autonomy of those individuals or groups designated to undertake these various activities. Management control systems include the protocols within firm structures that help deliver the strategy and include, for example, means of dictating how strategic planning is conducted and how other systems are introduced and operationalized idiosyncratically in the firm. Strategic planning systems are perhaps the most important systems an organization can implement. Put simply, a robust strategic planning system enables the firm to formulate strategies and action plans that will help it achieve profitability and sustainability.

The governance dimension of the framework's organizational level is built on the idea that there must be concurrent focus on business governance and family governance. This will be dictated by the organizational life cycle of the business and the generation of the family. For the family determined to continue, governance is a means to protect the family wealth and preserve the family legacy, for generations to come. Governance systems are used to direct and control an organization for and on behalf of the owners. They are built upon an interlocking framework of rules, relationships, structures, systems, and processes within and by which organizational authority is exercised and controlled. Understanding the unique governance dynamics of family business requires distinguishing between business governance and family governance.

The entrepreneurship dimension considers the need for entrepreneurial leadership and entrepreneurial strategy. To understand and explain entrepreneurship in family versus nonfamily businesses, the concept of entrepreneurial orientation (EO) is useful. The EO construct has five main dimensions: (i) innovativeness, (ii) proactivity, (iii) risk-taking, (iv) competitiveness, and (v) autonomy. Innovativeness is a firm's tendency to engage in and support new ideas, novelty, experimentation, and creative processes that result in new products, services, or technological processes. Proactivity refers to the propensity to compete aggressively and proactively with industry rivals. Risk-taking is about the tendency of a firm's top management to take risks related to investment decisions and strategic choices in the face of uncertainty. Competitiveness refers to the capacity to respond to market pressures. Autonomy relates to the intentional focus on remaining distinctive.

The stewardship dimension looks at the stewardship climate of the organization and stewardship orientation of the individual or family cohort. Stewards are intrinsically motivated, use personal rather than positional power, and see the business as an extension of themselves. They develop family and business climates that are identifiable through their collectivist culture, low power distance, and involvement orientation. They are the polar opposites of the corporate psychopaths earlier introduced. Recall that stewardship theory is one of the keystone theoretical approaches.

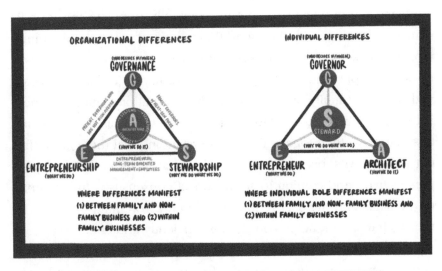

Illustration 19 FAMILY HETEROGENEITY FRAMEWORKS

Tactical Meta-Framework

At the individual level, the steward is paramount to continuity. The architect concept depicts the leader as someone who understands the need to introduce appropriate structures, particularly during times of transition. The governor is well-equipped to take on governing roles both in the family and the business, and the entrepreneur understands that entrepreneurship, really, is that which will enable the enterprising family to continue differently.

Four Rs Framework

When the family enterprise member who introduced me to the four Rs framework told me that 90% of his angst related to family members went away when he committed to populating the four Rs matrix, I knew it was something that I needed to understand and share. Like many of the 20 other frameworks in this book, the 4 Rs framework is simple. It's fundamental. But like many of the others, it has been overly complicated, often appearing in books or research articles in an unnecessarily convoluted form. That's not meant to be disparaging, but rather to reflect reality.

I encourage you to draw and eventually populate the four Rs matrix, in keeping with the broad theme here of using simple frameworks to make complex conversations easier. It is also a good answer to offer people who are beginning a governance journey or tasked with writing a family protocol or family constitution, when they inevitably ask, "Where do we start?" A good place to start is by populating this matrix. Getting together and understanding that there are different perspectives, becoming accomplished at hearing other people's perspectives, and coming to some sort of consensus is fundamental to the skills and mindset required to build a continuity model. The four Rs framework helps you do this efficiently and effectively.

The four Rs consist of role, requirement, responsibility, and remuneration. These form the first row of the matrix, as labels.

The first column of the matrix (i.e. role), is driven, not surprisingly, by the three circles framework in that the roles of focus are owner, director, executive or employee, and family member.

With four roles broken into three dimensions, the 4 Rs framework has 12 cells to populate (Illustration 20). Populating these cells looks simple but isn't, if done carefully and well. Populating them intentionally, authentically, and consultatively will require commitment to process and intuitive tweaking. It takes time, as each of the open cells requires robust debate. There is no one way to go about this. Some who have governance structures in place find that this is a good exercise in helping them to, in one simple matrix, replicate their full constitution, protocol, or subsections of those documents. Moreover, it is a worthwhile endeavor for siblings commencing the governance journey. It is an even more worthwhile endeavor for a cousin consortium charged with writing and/or championing a family and business governance agenda.

The example provided in the figure gives you one way to consider populating the cells but is by no means the only way. The key is to make it simple. The optimal approach is to have the detail in some other document, while filling in the matrix to be readily producible and replicable. The real test, as with most ideas here, is to be able to tell the story on a napkin.

When asked "For whom is this framework useful?" the answer is easy. Pick a stakeholder and you will immediately see why having a simple, populated four Rs framework will benefit their understanding. For example, a person recruited to join a family business in an executive role may think that its family-owned nature will mean a deficit of role clarity. Put them at ease by reproducing or sharing with them the completed four Rs framework. Similarly, a potential director asked to join the board, whether a well-established or nascent board, will appreciate, upon being shown the four Rs, that there is an effort to ensure that family roles are understood and that the potential for tension or conflict due to family involvement or med-dling is reduced through better understanding of the roles people play. For affines, this tool is critical as they need to understand that there are specific roles and activities they can and cannot engage in, particularly those related to ownership if ownership is for bloodline family members only. It is also useful for next-generation members who need to know the expectations set for them about joining their business. They will benefit from understanding this at an early stage. Many see a role in the business as a birthright. Using the four Rs to explain to them that a role as an employee or executive comes with requirements, responsibility, and appropriate, market-set remunera-tion, helps to professionalize and enables them to strategize their way forward in a manner consistent with continuity.

Overall, the four Rs, simple in its appearance but complex in its development and implementation, is as important as any of the other frameworks introduced in this meta-framework; it has relevance to all concepts here and is fundamental in developing the full plans that will be introduced as part of the Continuity Canvas. Thus, working

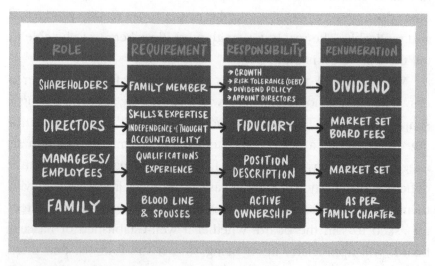

Illustration 20 FOUR Rs FRAMEWORK

seriously on the population of this matrix is a primary first step in the development of your canvas.

Four Strategy Dimensions Framework

Strategy is a big topic, and strategic planning is one of the four plans that make up the Continuity Canvas. The four strategy dimensions included in Kaplan and Norton's balanced scorecard approach provide an effective way for anyone involved in family enterprise to understand the vast strategic management and strategic process conversations required. Library shelves are jam-packed with information about strategic management. Office buildings are full of consultants well-equipped and eager to develop and help implement a strategic plan. Reviewing in great detail what these books say and what these folks do would waste valuable space here.

Much more important is to consider what strategy is and how it manifests. Simply put, strategy is understanding where you are, where you want to go to, and how you are going to get there. The balanced scorecard approach has as its center the vision and the mission of the entity. The four dimensions of the scorecard are customer perspective, financial perspective, innovation and learning perspective, and internal business perspective. For each of these perspectives there need to be established objective measures and targets; typically, there are three objectives for each of these perspectives. The objectives begin with the word "to" written simply so that everybody can understand what it is they are required to do. How those objectives are measured needs to be established so there is clear and articulated accountability for each of the three objectives and the targets will be agreed-upon performance metrics, which also indicate who is going to do what. The beauty of this approach is that it looks fundamentally at lead indicators, but the other key distinction of this scorecard or any scorecard that you elect to develop is that it

69

enables a lot of information to be shared efficiently and evaluations can be made on an ongoing basis whether objectives are missing. As well, each of the objectives articulated have direct links to the vision and the mission. So, the scorecard is a valuable management and measurement tool that ensures that what counts gets counted; in continuity modeling it's closely linked to strategic planning. The scorecard is not negotiable and must be treated as a priority. Later, we introduce the concept of a quadruple bottom-line scorecard to capture the focal dimensions of continuity (Illustration 21).

A related conversation centers on decision-making. A useful way to consider how better decisions are made is to consider that most if not all begin with a thesis, i.e. a worldview, a conjecture. The complementary opposite is the antithesis whereby alternatives are considered. With both tabled, a decision is arrived at by the *synthesis* of the thesis and the antithesis.

The antithesis should throw up alternatives and a recommendation will emerge. The quality of this process is dependent on the pundits, particularly those involved in the antithesis brainstorm. An interesting view on this is offered by those who study what is referred to as disinterested dialogue. They claim that, while typically a great deal of time is usually spent in the analysis phase of a key decision, from the collection of an extensive amount of information, to its financial analysis, to the construction of projections about future scenarios, internal and external analysts often engage in collecting and analyzing evidence compiled in thick reports. However, very little time is spent on the art of constructing stronger approaches to discuss the evidence collected and its analysis, entering into a candid dialogue about the assumptions behind the projections, and possible alternative explanations and options (i.e. *antithesis* and *synthesis*). Of course, a robust analysis (i.e. *thesis*) should also test assumptions, alternative explanations, and various options. However, studies suggest that this is not sufficient for an effective decision; teams of executives that engage in a *disinterested dialogue* of the decision are more likely to perform these tasks than to simply rely on the analysis itself. Disinterested dialogue is defined as a fact-based and transparent dialogue about the analysis performed that addresses the major uncertainties of the strategic decision as part of the companie's existing portfolio of decisions. Common sense would also suggest that groups with multiple areas of expertise and experience are better positioned to perform the type of reflective judgment required to build an appropriate antithesis. In fact, during disinterested dialogue, individuals have the opportunity to place their knowledge into a broader context and are less likely to overvalue their prior experience; they are also more likely to engage in critical thinking by questioning assumptions, evaluating evidence, and testing the logic of ideas, proposals, and suggested course of actions that are part of strategic decisions. It is this process that is a key distinguishing factor in how successful multigenerational families in business make decisions differently.

In other words, a *thesis* is established using "robustness of analysis" construct, an *antithesis* is developed using "disinterested dialogue" measures, *synthesis* is the result of decision-makers blending the thesis and antithesis, or what could be termed "negating the negated." The *broad* argument is that families have different decision-making processes due to the influence of the dual, independent and interdependent, family and business systems. Decision-makers charged with continuation-related decisions in family firms are influenced by family-linked idiosyncratic factors. Included in these are such factors as founder centrality, family involvement and influence, time horizons, balance sheet considerations, risk profiles, debt attitude, financial and non-financial metrics, as well as stakeholder relationships that would differ from the norm. The *specific* argument is that decision-makers, charged with managing family and business systems concurrently, develop their *thesis* (measured by the degree of

71

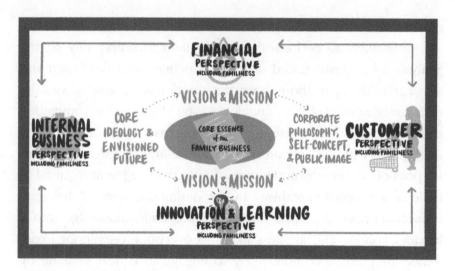

Illustration 21 FOUR STRATEGY DIMENSIONS FRAMEWORK

robust analysis) differently, which would reason that the challenge (i.e. the negation) to the thesis, the *antithesis* (established by measuring disinterested dialogue) would also be established differently, and as a result "negating the negated" (i.e. *synthesis*) would result in different (not necessarily better or worse) outcomes.

Fundamental Meta-Framework

Clarity around, and commitment to, the four frameworks that make up the fundamental meta-framework is paramount. Without this clarity and commitment, use of the other five meta-frameworks will likely not gain traction.

Four Trust Dimensions

Trust underpins everything. My observations of countless family enterprises have confirmed that without an understanding of trust there is a limited chance of continuity. Like all big topics, trust must be broken down. The trust literature, not surprisingly, is vast, but what is agreed on is that there are four dimensions of trust. Multiple research projects I've worked on in recent years confirm this, as does my own personal understanding of and experience with trust. The four trust dimensions are integrity, ability, benevolence, and consistency, as summarized below:

- **Integrity**: the quality of being good; having strong moral principles; moral uprightness.
- **Ability**: the possession of the means or skill to do something.
- **Benevolence**: the desire to do good for others; goodwill; charitableness.
- **Consistency**: the quality of always behaving or performing in a similar way.

When shared with practitioners, students, and others, these dimensions pass what we Australians call the "pub test": they are quickly of intuitive appeal, once explained. The best way to establish this is to ask an individual to "think of someone that you don't trust"; then, after a short time follow up with, "I'll now tell you why you don't trust that person." Every single time, the reason that person is not trusted will have something to do with one of these four dimensions. As we did for the Adizes leadership and life stage framework presented earlier, you can adopt a configuration approach by using a capital or lowercase letter to represent that the reason the focal person is not trusted is due to their lack of integrity, ability, benevolence, and/or consistency. Along with asking someone else, try carrying out the exercise for yourself by thinking of someone you don't trust. I guarantee you will quickly be able to establish why you don't trust someone, and the reasons will fall into one or more of those categories.

You could also do the exercise with yourself as the untrusted individual. Consider honestly why someone may have had reason not to trust you, and then apply a capital or lowercase I, A, B, or C (Illustration 22). When doing this exercise with others I like to keep the I (integrity) constant, because I assume that anyone in their network will have integrity, or they wouldn't associate with them in the first place.

The next key question in this exercise and in any trust-related discussion is "Can you rebuild trust?" Considering the three dimensions other than integrity, if you believe someone doesn't have the ability needed, that may be challenging to improve, especially by you. Moreover, it's hard to say definitively whether you can change someone's benevolence. But it may be about *perceived* benevolence, and that's something you can bring to their attention: specifically, that they appear inwardly focused and not contributing to the collective.

Regarding consistency, that is a behavior that can potentially be addressed.

Another way to frame trust is to understand the definition of trustworthiness as "a willingness to be vulnerable." The best example of this that I've heard was not intentionally related to this topic: a sage family business leader explained to me that the two most important words in the English language are "help me." He went on to describe how he used these words to get people committed to something he was trying to achieve. But what he was saying, and that he didn't realize he was saying, is that using the words "help me" was a way to demonstrate his vulnerability or the preparedness and willingness to be vulnerable, which is the definition of trustworthiness as noted above. Saying "help me," or words to that effect, signifies that you are building a bridge between yourself and another person, demonstrating that you are vulnerable, which, by definition, builds trust.

Another way to frame this is by saying that you know your perspective on a particular issue but that you want to understand the perspectives and positions of others. Again, it is a way of demonstrating that you are vulnerable and open, which is a way of facilitating trust-building. This relates directly to, or can be used to boost, many of the activities of the 21 frameworks and 6 meta-frameworks.

The aim of the game, which I observed John Ward reinforce at every opportunity in his writing and presentations, is to build trust "in a team of decision-making teams" and to answer the simple question "Are we in good hands?," or to extend that to "Do we trust those in decision-making roles to make appropriate decisions on our behalf?"

Trust is the backbone of society and fundamental to any *Continuity Model Generation* conversation. As a family business leader, who is a continuity model exemplar shared, "Without trust, you have nothing." Motivated by this observation, and an increasing appreciation of the role of trust, my current research is unbundling the *ability*

Illustration 22 FOUR TRUST DIMENSIONS

dimension to reveal a finer grained understanding, which considers the aspects of *cap*ability, *vulner*ability, and *malle*ability. How trust is built is also of interest in these studies, as is the stability of the dimensions over time. Expect this to evolve into a Trust Canvas with multiple configurations.

Five-Stage Life Cycle Framework

Organizational researchers have proposed multiple life cycle models.

Most models are multistage in nature, comprised of three to ten stages, and describe a similar pattern of development of organizations. Models with more stages seem to break down general stages to rather specific developmental periods, while models with fewer, broader stages integrate two or more developmental periods for the sake of parsimony. In addition, some distinguish between small organizations and organizations in general. The five-stage framework based on the seminal work of Miller and Friesen (1984) is applicable to all organizations and is generally consistent with the body of literature on the topic. In it, organizations are theorized to evolve through five general stages: start-up, expansion, consolidation, diversification, and decline.

The five-stage framework proposed by Lester, Parnell, and Carraher (2003) is comprehensive yet parsimonious, so it fits perfectly for continuity modelers. This model bears important differences relative to existing five-stage models. First, it is not designed only for small businesses, nor is it designed exclusively for larger corporate entities; the framework is relevant to all organizations. It accomplishes this relevance by incorporating the best features from several leading models (Illustration 23). Here are descriptions of each stage:

Stage One: Existence

Considered the entrepreneurial or birth stage, existence marks the beginning of organizational development. The focus here is on viability, or simply identifying and gaining a sufficient number of customers to support the organization's existence. Decision-making and ownership are in the hands of one, or a few, and the environment is considered to be unanalyzable. Organizations in this stage tend to enact or create their own environments.

Stage Two: Survival

As firms move into the survival stage, they seek to develop some formalization of structure and establish their own distinctive competencies (Miller and Friesen 1984). In this stage, goals are formulated, with the primary objective being the generation of enough revenue to continue operations and finance sufficient growth to stay competitive.

Stage Three: Success

Commonly called maturity, the success stage represents an organizational form where formalization and control through bureaucracy are the norm. A common problem in this stage is "red tape" (Miller and Friesen 1984), or, having to wade through layers of organizational structure to get anything accomplished. That's partly because job descriptions, policies and procedures, and hierarchical reporting relationships have become much more formal. Such organizations have passed the survival test, growing to a point where they may seek to protect what they have gained instead of targeting new territory. The top management team focuses on planning and strategy, leaving daily operations to middle managers.

Stage Four: Renewal

The renewing organization displays a desire to return to a leaner time (Miller and Friesen 1984) when collaboration and teamwork fostered innovation and creativity. This creativity is sometimes facilitated through the use of a matrix structure, and decision-making is highly decentralized. The organization is still large and bureaucratic, but organizational members are encouraged to work within the bureaucracy without adding complexity to it. The needs of customers are placed above those of organizational members.

Stage Five: Decline

Although firms may exit the life cycle at any stage, the decline stage can reflect and/or trigger their demise. This stage is characterized by politics and power (Mintzberg 1984), as organizational members become more concerned with personal goals than with organizational goals. For some organizations, the inability to meet the external demands of a former stage has led them to a period of decline where

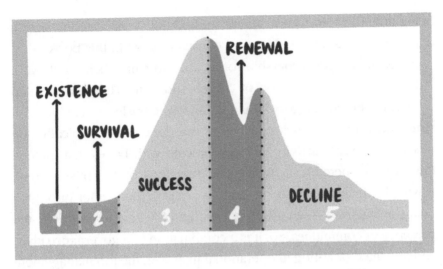

Illustration 23 FIVE-STAGE LIFE CYCLE FRAMEWORK

they experience lack of profitability and loss of market share (Miller and Friesen 1984). Control and decision-making tend to return to a handful of people, as the desire for power and influence in earlier stages has eroded the organization's viability.

Regardless of their organization's life cycle stage, continuity modelers must understand how to create and capture value, as part of their purview. The four ways to drive true value are through different types of engineering, specifically, operating engineering, financial engineering, governance engineering, and multiples arbitrage (market timing, multiples expansion).

Church and State Framework

Continuity modeling, in general, requires storytelling, and the church and state framework facilitates the narrative that there is a separation between family activities and business activities. This is important, as has been stressed throughout these pages. Moreover, multiple stakeholders need to demonstrate their understanding of the landscape by being able to reproduce a significant body of work into one simple diagram, a necessary skill set and constant theme in this book.

The family and ownership forms and structures belong above a dotted line in any depiction of church and state. These are labeled under the church category, while the multiple business activities and structural forms are included below the dotted line. Typically, the business, or state, activity will be depicted with boxes that include the various operating activities and functions of the business(es). It will also include how these entities are governed either through a board of directors or an advisory board and, where appropriate, the presence of committees. So, it is a combination of a governance chart and an edited or abridged operational map with the top management team in their various functions (Illustration 24).

The family activities and forums will be found above the dotted line. This will be a combination of ownership structures and governance processes in place to govern the owners and the family. This constellation of activities includes, for example, the family assembly, family office, family council, philanthropic activities, and committees attached to any of those; all family shareholdings, where appropriate, can also be included.

It is also possible to demonstrate the flow of revenues and profits in simple form. Typically, this would include some sort of line to channel profits from the business, or state, below the dotted line up into the family and ownership, or church, above the dotted line. One hundred percent would be shown to be distributed from the state to the church, initially. The church would then systematically, diagrammatically, or figuratively distribute a portion of that 100% back to the state, and distribute the balance as dividends to owners, funds to the family office for various activities, and investments away from the legacy business or core operating business and into philanthropic and other activities. So, though this sounds very simplistic, it is in fact an incredibly useful framework that can tell multiple

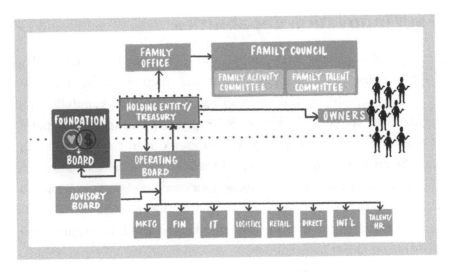

Illustration 24 CHURCH AND STATE FRAMEWORK

stories and depict how divergent family enterprise activities relate. For example, in the family that shared this approach with me, 100% of the operating business's income is channeled to a family treasury, then 15% of that money is distributed as dividends, 60% is distributed back to the business for operating funds, and 25% is distributed to the family office to develop a portfolio of assets separate to the core legacy industry activities as a risk-minimization strategy; the assets include long-term bonds, some real estate assets, share portfolios for the business, and technology investments (e.g. joint ventures), among others.

Also included below the line, in the state or business section of this framework, are the governance structures to operate the legacy business activities. So much can be told by carefully constituting a church and state governance framework. As is important for many stakeholders, the framework is easy for many to understand, even if they are not conversant with the operations of the business, which makes the tool vital and pivotal for ensuring that people understand what it takes to deliver continuity and engage in the same.

Four Innovation Capabilities

Innovation capability is dependent on a confluence of factors. The four we consider in this framework are corralled under the categories of technology-driven (i.e. technology development capability and operations capability) and business-driven (i.e. management capability and transaction capability). Technology-driven capabilities facilitate the creation of new products as well as the processes that enable the manufacture of these products on a commercial scale. Business-driven capabilities synchronize the integration and coordination of technology-driven capabilities (Zawislak, et al. 2012) (Illustration 25). Let's take a closer look at each.

Technology Development Capabilities

Technology development capability is mostly concerned with how firms offer new products. It involves movements of the production function with the outcome of the associated learning being products and services with new technical patterns. Technology development is more than technological change, as the major goal is to provide innovative solutions to the market.

Operations capability is the ability to efficiently operate the technology, to produce tradable goods and services. Operations capability is therefore process-focused and includes activities such as quality control, preventative maintenance, workflow, and inventory control. Firm knowledge is inextricably linked to processes of production and the subsequent capabilities emerging from the dynamism associated with learning by doing. Given the additional contribution operations capability makes vis-à-vis aligning production strategy with strategic imperatives, operations capability is also a result of selecting competitive priorities in order to take advantage of valuable efficiencies related to, for example, low cost, quality, delivery time, responsiveness, and flexibility. As such, the domain of operations capability encompasses contributing to strategic advantage through processes that deliver continuous cost-reduction, quality improvement, strategic flexibility, and stakeholder responsiveness.

Business-Driven Capabilities

Management capability is concerned with the maintenance of smooth information flows and outputs in order to achieve higher efficiency rates. This capability, therefore, is more general in focus than, say, operations capability. Where the focus for operations capability is on processes that develop in tandem with technological-capability-based routines to deliver efficiencies, management capability requires taking action and responding appropriately in situations where technology fails to be perfectly routinized. In increasingly complex and unpredictable environments, where problem-solving and decision-making have unprecedented reliance on imperfect information, management capability requires a repertoire of skills that must be applied

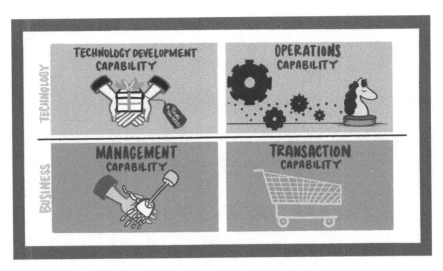

Illustration 25 FOUR INNOVATION CAPABILITIES FRAMEWORK

flexibly. For example, management capability necessitates innovative responses to reduce costs resulting from uncertainty; concurrently, management capability is linked to the continual adjustment of administrative structures and orchestration of resources. As such, management capability combines continuity with innovation.

Transaction capability facilitates the sale of the product or service. Advantage accrues to firms that innovate transaction capability because the new products created through technology capability, produced efficiently through processes introduced in operations capability in a firm in which all areas are tuned and running smoothly by capable management, will be transacted economically because marketing, bargaining, and delivery costs are reduced.

Part II

The Continuity Canvas

At this point it is important to reinforce two aspects of Continuity Modeling. First, the *Continuity Model Generation* process, at its core, is intended to broaden and deepen any accepted approaches currently employed by business-owning families. This, therefore, suggests that the process is open for interpretation but also that if you find yourself following the same well-worn path and having the same conversations, stop. Consider this process a longer-term-oriented perspective powered by theory-driven, evidence-based frameworks. And think of your ultimate audience, and the beneficiaries of your prescience, as your children's children.

The second aspect to reinforce is that your continuity model is *your* continuity model. How you construct this will be determined by a confluence of factors. The 21 frameworks with their 87 dimensions are yours to own, interpret, and apply. Approach this ownership, interpretation, and application with the knowledge that getting lost in the weeds will be distracting and defeat the overall intent. This, again, distinguishes this approach from the "traditional." Another way to say this is that developing a Continuity Model Canvas will, among other things, enable owner-stewards, family-stewards, and manager-stewards *to broaden and deepen their thinking*. This broadening and deepening of thought contributes to decision-making processes that are more robust and sustainable and which will be captured in a living document that is crucial to align interests and behavior.

Strategy:
Strategic Planning for Continuity

Cornerstone Concept: Design a Quadruple Bottom-Line Scorecard.

Preamble: Here's how to look at strategic planning: knowing where you are, where you want to go to, and deciding among options for the best way to get there. Simple is best. But the simplicity masks the complexity. Deciding on objectives, measures, and targets sounds much easier than it is. And then consider that you need to do this for operating businesses, liquid assets, real estate holdings, and philanthropic activities. Deciding who is going to do what by when is vital for continuity. But integrating multiple strategic plans is exponentially complex.

Strategic Planning for Continuity I: Collecting and Collating Basic Information

Chances are that most readers will be familiar with or have engineered something akin to a strategic plan for the main operating business. Whatever form this has taken is not of much concern, as long as it brings clarity and accountability to the decision-making process, particularly as it relates to direction. What is less likely is that the same "plan" or planning process exists for anything other than the main operating business. And this does not make sense to continuity modelers. As such, strategic plans and the strategic planning process is a fundamental focus of the *Continuity Model Generation*.

There are plenty (read: too many) books and experts that communicate the basic principles of strategic planning. No point in using valuable space and time to re-tread that well-traveled path. Rather, look to the frameworks for guidance.

The main thing to remember for this conversation is that strategic planning is in place to reduce the potential for tension between the manager–stewards and owner–stewards (and by extension, the family–stewards). Recall the three circles framework. The managers (i.e. those charged with managing on behalf of the owners or family) need to know with some level of confidence what it is that they are managing and in what direction each of these entities or activities is heading. Disregard that this seems simplistic, because even those who are in daily contact with the many commercial activities in their family enterprises will admit that it is a constant challenge to keep on top of things.

There is no one way to build your Continuity Canvas. But a good place to start is by becoming familiar with the commercial activities for which strategic planning is required. Start by making a list. Include (i) core business(es), (ii) joint venture businesses, (iii) partnerships, (iv) real estate assets in multiple categories (e.g. commercial, land, retail), (v) liquid assets (e.g. cash holdings or reserves, shares, bonds), and (vi) philanthropic activities. That should cover most of it, but there may be others that are more nuanced, such as co-operative arrangements, franchisee–franchisor agreements, and long-term property leases, for example. If you are not convinced that making such a list is a good idea for the enterprise, do it for your own nuclear family and/or the assets you personally own. For example, you'd list your house, holiday condo, vehicles, cash in the bank, and the like. Once familiar with the general process, multi-generational families often follow Continuity Canvas methodology to understand and share within their nuclear family how their assets are arranged.

The Continuity Generation appreciates that for each of these "activities," eventually, there must be a clear understanding of the basic condition of the portfolio represented: returns expected, investments anticipated, growth and/or exit intentions, and so on.

After compiling the list, which will likely be enlightening in itself for many, crudely rank-order the items from top priority to lowest. This is not an exact science, and don't sweat the details or argue over them. To make it easier, establish a critical metric, which could be financial contribution or the potential for tension. Typically, the key business activity is a top priority, and the others cascade down.

Next, honestly evaluate how robust or professional the strategic planning process is for the key business activity. Usually, if the founder is still the controlling owner, there is a good chance that the strategic planning process is very much as that person dictates. Entrepreneurs are not known for their "strategic" planning. That is not a fight you want to get into at this point. It is not an abnormal problem. But, if there is commitment to continuity, at some point this founder issue will need to be addressed. Also avoid getting into the weeds. If there is concerted effort to improve the strategic planning process in the key business activity, this will likely mean that other activities will benefit through a type of "spillover" effect.

Call the process what you want (the Continuity Generation is not big on MBA-speak), a situational analysis, an asset snapshot, a business activity registry. . .It doesn't matter. Remember, moreover, that many of those who are part of this conversation are there for the first time. The challenge is to make it attractive enough for them to care. Openness and transparency rule the day. But best to paint with a thick brush.

What may be becoming clear is that for this and the other planning processes, you will need a plan of attack. After reviewing the guidelines included here, spend the time to digest the information and craft your approach. Discuss with others. Not to complicate the issue, but what is really needed is a strategic approach for the strategic planning process, in other words, a *strategic plan plan*.

As you ponder this, consider that the process of strategic planning in its simplest form (or as most members of the continuity generation suggest, make it so that you can explain it to a ten-year-old relative) is about having a shared vision (i.e. what we are trying to accomplish or where we are trying to go), then articulating a mission that is an action statement that provides additional clarity on how the vision is going to be achieved, and then establishing some clear objectives, measures and targets.

Here are three steps that are helpful in developing an approach plan for the strategic plan within the Continuity Canvas (Illustration 26):

1. List as many relevant commercial activities as you can.
2. Prioritize the list of activities using an agreed-upon metric.
3. Rate the current level of strategic planning sophistication on a ten-point scale from "desperately needs work" (one) to "best practice" (ten).

This could first be done independently and then together with family as a point of discussion. You could also do the planning as part of a workshop, which will highlight among other things (i) how much there is to know, (ii) how little is known, and (iii) the importance of not only having a strategic plan for the various activities in question but also to have a plan for the strategic planning process,

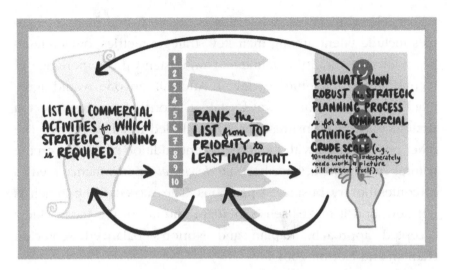

Illustration 26 THREE-STEP APPROACH PLAN FOR THE STRATEGIC PLAN

particularly in the formative period of getting the collective to commit to continuity modeling.

Strategic Planning for Continuity II: Cornerstone Concept Equals a Quadruple-Bottom-Line Scorecard

The information collected and collated in the first stage above should be enlightening; but it is the second stage of strategic planning for continuity that truly catapults the conversation forward. The cornerstone concept to have in mind here is a quadruple-bottom-line scorecard. That implies two key aspects: (i) quadruple and (ii) scorecard. Keeping consistent with broadening traditional approaches and a longer-term orientation, the fourth dimension added to the plan on top of financial, social, and environmental, is that related to talent. While this is not new, and many companies include talent among their key strategic metrics, owner–families with a continuity commitment understand the importance of recruiting and retaining key talent. After all, anyone would agree that there is an ongoing "war for talent." Considering this aspect, a strategic objective ensures that it is included in all discourse. The other bottom lines, with the more recent addition of a focus on the natural environment, have become *de rigueur* performance metrics in contemporary business operations. The scorecard approach is not new, and it makes sense to adapt and adopt the most widely accepted approach: Kaplan and Norton's balanced scorecard (Kaplan and Norton 2001).

The overarching objective is to develop a strategic planning process for continuity that is driven by the 21 frameworks as they apply to financial, social, environmental, and talent performance metrics. Recall from the balanced scorecard overview in the tactical meta-framework that the four "balanced" dimensions are financial, customer, innovation and learning, and internal process. This widely accepted management and measurement tool is ideal for strategic operation planning conversations. The broader perspectives in the continuity model of financial, social, environmental, and talent are obviously more in line with continuity and longer-horizon thinking and acting.

The first task is to consider which of the 21 frameworks will assist in considering how to populate the 4 perspectives. Illustrated Table 1 provides an example, followed by more detailed explanations in the text. Keep in mind that we could have included other specifics to enhance or replace these.

Financial	Keystone: Agency; Owner-steward; Manager-steward Familial: Issues are Same, Perspectives Differ Individual: Persuasiveness Generational: Affordable Loss Tactical: Financial Perspective of the Balanced Scorecard (BSC) Fundamental: Business = State
Social	Keystone: Social Logic Familial: Commitment to Us Individual: Organizational Stewardship Generational: Learn Our Family Business (L2) Tactical: Customer Fundamental: Family = Church
Environmental	Keystone: Resource-based View Familial: Philanthropy Leader Individual: Organizational Stewardship Generational: Learn to Lead (L3) Tactical: Innovation & Learning Fundamental: Technology Development Capability
Talent	Keystone: Principal Cost Familial: Community Individual: Four Tests Framework Generational: Learn Business; Learn Our Family Business (L1,2) Tactical: Four Rs Framework Fundamental: Four Trust Dimensions Framework; Business-Driven Capabilities

Illustrated Table 1 POPULATING THE FOUR PERSPECTIVES USING THE FRAMEWORKS

Financial Perspective

- **Objective:** To ensure long-term financial health.
- **Measures:** ROI; ROIC; ROE; Revenue from new business; Patents.
- **Targets:** Comparable to, or better than, industry average.

Keystone Meta-Framework: Agency, Owner–Steward, and Manager–Steward

Considering that long-term financial health is the objective for this perspective, aspects of agency theory and the three circles framework are relevant. But all four theories have relevance. Agency theory considers that principals appoint agents to act on their behalf. The business's long-term financial health will be predicated on those agents' alignment with the stated objective. Whether the agents are board members, the CEO, the top management team, or line staff, it's important that they have a clear understanding that, in this case, the objective of financial health over the long term is critical. Short-termism is to be avoided. Investments and decisions are made with a longer-term orientation, and patient capital must be not only tolerated but encouraged. As well, there is a need to guard strictly against opportunistic plays by agents with access to superior information. Associated with this are incentive schemes to retain aligned agents. A key notion of the agency–stewardship comparison, and a common theme throughout, is that agents should act as stewards who are more intrinsically than extrinsically motivated, see the business as an extension of themselves, and are involvement-oriented. This confirms the appropriateness of the three circles framework to further understand how the stated objective (of long-term financial health) is front and center in the thinking and actions of stakeholders.

Further, manager–stewards are responsible for managing on behalf of the owners. While the activities under their custodianship are from multiple asset classes, their needs to be a shared understanding that while some investments may have a shorter time horizon (and often higher expected rate of return), the investment philosophy must be framed to align with long-term financial health. This will involve constant vigilance by manager–stewards, and their advisors, related to the balancing of the portfolio to ensure that risk is manageable, and exposure is balanced.

The additional granularity that we included in the family–steward circle of the three circles considered the utility heterogeneity of owners and also assists in interpreting the financial perspective of strategic planning for continuity. Recall the continuum anchored by economic and psychological returns. Again, with long-term financial health being the stated, agreed-upon objective, in the continuity model there should be an expectation that family–stewards figuratively congregate at the end of the continuum whereby, although they expect economic returns, it is also in their interest to understand that long-term financial health may require the need for the business in some years to retain more earnings at the expense of owners' dividends.

Familial Meta-Framework: Issues are the Same, Perspectives Differ

The familial meta-framework houses many dimensions that can be commissioned to add texture to the understanding of the financial perspective of strategic planning for continuity. The one that stands out comes from the RIPCC framework, specifically, the I, or issues.

Even more specifically, the idea that the issues are the same, but the perspectives are different. While it would be ideal to have everyone in the family committed to whatever it takes to ensure long-term financial health, the reality is, that will not likely happen. The reasons for this are many. For example, it may be that the whole continuity modeling approach does not sit well with everyone. Or it may be that historical family conflict impedes securing commitment to these types of decisions. It could be that affines are influencing the agenda in some way, such as having higher expectations related to "their" financial returns.

The list goes on, and rather than avoiding discussing the challenge, it's best for stakeholders to approach these issues head-on.

A good way to address this is through a polarity mapping exercise. This will involve understanding that some will be happy with a smaller dividend if it contributes to the enterprise's long-term health, while others will hold a diametrically opposed view, for one of the reasons mentioned above. The process then involves looking at the upside and downside of both perspectives. After going through this process, which ensures that different perspectives have been voiced and heard, the goal is to move forward with a strategy that can satisfy both viewpoints. In other words, it is not an "either–or" but a "both–and" approach.

A good way to consider how to break an impasse that is inevitable when viewpoints differ is to live by the mantra "disagree then commit." What this effectively means is that you understand that the chances of persuading everyone to agree is slight but that the process of getting input is what matters most. In addition, an understanding that a total commitment to the decision is paramount. Anything less will risk eventual sabotage.

Individual Meta-Framework: Persuasiveness

The persuasive mapping (persuasiveness) dimension of the servant leadership framework describes the extent to which leaders use sound reasoning and mental frameworks. Leaders high in persuasive mapping are skilled at mapping issues and conceptualizing greater possibilities, along with being compelling when articulating these opportunities. They encourage others to visualize the organization's future and are persuasive in securing actionable commitment to bring it to life; they are not coercive or manipulative. These capabilities may help them convince others whose perspectives are not aligned with longer-term horizons as they relate to financial expectations. A key to any discussion is to be prepared to persuade and be persuadable.

Generational Meta-Framework: Affordable Loss

One of the principles in Sarasvathy's effectual reasoning approach relates to financial perspectives. Specifically, she considers that entrepreneurs don't focus on how much money they are going to make, but rather on how much they *can afford to lose*. This is cogent advice when considering the long-term financial health of the business activities relevant to the strategic planning for continuity process. The fundamental mindset shift that this thinking involves would accommodate focus on embracing managed risk to ensure that, as the Millers describe, the business remains "spry." While not necessarily applicable to the full gamut of business activities, maintaining that the objective is to do what it takes to ensure long-term financial health should counter any tendency toward excessive conservatism. In fact, any of the many dimensions that consider entrepreneurship and/or innovation, either directly or indirectly, should be considered relevant when developing consensus around what it will take to deliver financial health over the long term, and consequently, continue.

Tactical Meta-Framework: Financial Perspective of the Balanced Scorecard

The balanced scorecard is housed in the tactical meta-framework. It is fully worth circling back to consider the eloquence of this tool. The motivation to include the financial perspective specifically is to highlight that, although important, Kaplan and Norton's scorecard concept is built around the notion that financial perspective is necessary but not sufficient. The beauty of the balanced scorecard is the "balanced" approach that considers the four perspectives concurrently and in tandem. Thus, when considering the broader and deeper approach associated with continuity modeling, it is opportune to reinforce that the financial perspective in this application is linked to the other three perspectives: social, environmental, and talent.

Fundamental Meta-Framework: Business Equals State

The financial perspective is predominantly a business perspective. Thus, it is considered part of the "state" in the church and state governance framework. One of the features of the church and state approach is that it tracks the flow of funds. Profits from the business activities are channeled from the state to the church for distribution. In a continuity model, the funds required for business activities take priority, then funds for family office activities (associated with diversifying risk from core business activities), then dividends for owners. The needs of the business therefore take precedence in the financial perspective, with a stated objective of long-term financial health. If the pendulum swings too much away from this and toward, for example, a priority on dividends for owners, there is a potential disconnect.

Continuity modeling is predicated on healthy profits, retained for growth and innovation rather than for rewarding owners excessively. Thus, a frugal dividend policy with additional "special" dividend years is preferred to an inflated percentage of profits being siphoned off. It just doesn't make sense not to first reinvest funds into core business activities and diversification. Embracing this idea may, when combined with other dimensions elaborated above, convince naysayers that if continuity is the ultimate goal and the stated objective is long-term financial health, the approach is a no-brainer.

Social Perspective

- **Objective:** To contribute as a united family to society.

- **Measures:** Impact; profits distributed to communities in which we operate; family involvement in community activities; promoting family as the fundamental social value creator; shared resources for community education; and pro bono hours.

- **Targets:** Annual positive impact improvement of X%; X% of profits committed by Year 20XX; and half of workforce engaged.

Keystone Meta-Framework: Social Logic

Transgenerational business-owning families typically understand the importance of doing well *and* doing good. The complementary logics framework keeps this in constant focus, with emphasis on the creation of socioeconomic wealth, not just economic wealth. This involves trade-offs, as too much focus on financial returns at the expense of committing to social aspects is as unsustainable as the inverse, or excessive commitment to social aspects, which could jeopardize healthy financial returns. Importantly, social commitment conversations tend to be emotion-laden and must be approached with care. This brings into focus the need for education related to the commercial aspects of "doing business." Ways of contributing to society other than through financial gifts need to be considered. And this highlights the need for a strategic approach to this important contributor to continuity. At some point in the life of the business and the family there will come a time that a strategic plan must be developed to ensure that *impact* is the performance metric, rather than dollars spent, pro bono hours, or resources donated.

Familial Meta-Framework: Commitment to Us

The RIPCC best practice framework is enlightening for many reasons. For the purpose of understanding the social aspects of the strategic planning process, it highlights the need to include family as the key to a healthy society. Though this may seem like a stretch, aspirant business-owning families are, often unknowingly and unintentionally, role models in an increasingly complex society. By demonstrating their "commitment to us," they are communicating that, regardless of culture or context, family remains the foundation of a healthy society. Indeed, family is the fundamental social value creator, and business-owning families acknowledge their important role, which is a not an insignificant motivator to focus on continuity.

Individual Meta-Framework: Organizational Stewardship from the Four Servant Leadership Dimensions

Stewardship, not surprisingly, dominates this book's pages. Recall the organizational stewardship dimension of the servant leadership framework: the extent to which leaders prepare an organization to make a positive contribution to society through community development, programs, and outreach. Organizational stewardship involves an ethic or value that is related to taking responsibility for the wellbeing of the community and making sure that strategies and decisions reflect the commitment to give back and leave things better than found. Leaders also work to develop a community spirit in the workplace, one that is preparing to leave a positive legacy.

Generational Meta-Framework: Learn Our Family Business

Part I noted that the four Ls framework stands out amongst the broader collection for its usefulness and acceptability. L2, "learning our family business," was positioned as the most important of the four Ls. Recall the line that I encouraged readers to learn by heart and repeat verbatim at any opportunity. Specifically, L2 is where you *learn the value of values, and keep the philosophies, but not the detail, in order to continue differently.* This relates directly to the social perspective of the strategic planning process vis-à-vis the need to understand the value of values. The suggestion is that a major contributor to "success" to date has been translating values into value. And it is the social value this creates that equates, eventually, to economic value. It may not be a directly observable, immediate relationship between expended effort and return, but the effect is positive. The social capital built over time by the family into the business and the community is difficult, even impossible, to quantify, but supremely important. This needs to be understood, as it really is the "secret sauce." The key is for subsequent-to-the-founding generations to interpret these values and institutionalize them in the business and family. This challenge is encompassed with the second message in the learn-by-heart sentence: keep the philosophies, not the detail.

Tactical Meta-Framework: Customer

The customer perspective is one of the four perspectives of the balanced scorecard. It is included here as vital to the understanding of inclusion of social aspects in strategic planning for continuity because, increasingly, customers are influenced by much more than quality and price when making purchase decisions. The customer now values the *story* behind the product. Moreover, they have unprecedented access to creating and consuming this story through the many social media platforms available. Everyone understands this because everyone is a customer. How purchasers and users of products perceive the providers of these has never been more transparent, including who the providers are, where they source from, and many other dimensions. That means today's businesses have virtually nowhere to hide.

Managing this relationship is in everyone's purview. So, acknowledge this reality when developing a strategic plan for continuity. Overall, customers are key stakeholders in the family's ability to continue. They are also, therefore, vested in whether the business-owning family can deliver societal value. The connection may not always be top of mind and can be lost in the process, but it remains significant. That customers are included as one of the four balanced scorecard perspectives is arguably one of the reasons that the balanced scorecard has been so impactful as a management and measurement tool. Customers, in short, should have a seat at the table.

Fundamental Meta-Framework: Family Equals Church

The church in the church and state governance framework is a euphemism for family. While the financial conversation that preceded this section considered the state aspects of the framework, it makes sense to balance that approach by focusing the lens on the church or family to highlight family's role in society. This is consistent with the thread developed in the preceding six meta-frameworks and reinforces the value of approaching these conversations from multiple angles. While many of the social initiatives can be and are undertaken in the business activities, it is likely that the "big ticket" endeavors are pursued above the dotted line in "the church." It is here that a percentage of profits is allocated to two forums related directly to social impact through their focus on philanthropic contributions. Over time, this will likely manifest as a family foundation. The other forum that lives above the line is the one serving as the "family glue": the family council, which champions family activities. The council, for example, launches education programs that socialize current and future generations. An intentional focus on these forums, how they are financed, designed, and function, is important to the ability to fulfill any social agenda. Optimal social impact will not happen without this intentional focus.

At this juncture, it is worth reinforcing how a recurring theme is the interconnectedness of the different conversations herein, which highlights the practicality of the broadened perspective, a hallmark of continuity modeling. Do not fall into the trap of just reading the words on these pages; instead, connect the concepts in the sections. Remember, the interpretations included here are fundamentally my interpretation. I am ignorant to your specific circumstance and do not pretend to know your intimacies and intricacies. Only you, your family, and those close to you do. The real work happens when you add your voice to create your own narrative. Make it *your* Continuity Canvas.

If, at this point, you can feel some benefit in a broader and deeper way of thinking, manifest it by pursuing development of a quadruple-bottom-line scorecard (the cornerstone concept of the strategic planning process for continuity planning). That will help you take heart from a quick view down the track. Specifically, it will enable you to note the potential of the other three cornerstone concepts: developing an informed individual philosophy of stewardship, producing a handwritten personal legacy statement, and crafting the family's governance philosophy. The end result is like a big family network where everyone and everything seem related.

Environmental Perspective

- **Objective:** To preserve the natural environment for future generations.
- **Measures:** Carbon footprint; and sustainable energy use.
- **Targets:** Bettering best-practice targets; and 100% sustainable energy by the year 20XX.

Keystone Meta-Framework: Resource-Based View

One of the benefits of this book's approach — that is, introduce the 21 frameworks in Part I and bring them to life in Part II — is that it offers the opportunity to tease out key concepts in more detail over time. A case in point is employing the resource-based view, introduced briefly in Part I, to consider the environment perspective of the quadruple bottom-line. Recall that the thinking behind the Resource-Based View (RBV) approach is that companies have resources that they bundle idiosyncratically to develop capabilities. These capabilities, once identified, contribute to there being able to develop strategies that leverage these capabilities and contribute to sustaining competitive advantage. The resources are framed as VRIN: valuable, rare, imperfectly imitable, and non-substitutable. Related to attitudes toward the natural environment, this is where business-owners have a fundamental advantage, particularly those who are focused on continuity.

Recall the earlier point that decisions are made with your children's children in mind. That being the case, a cognizance about preserving the natural environment is crucial. Put another way, if companies pursue activities that pollute the water, taint the air, and/or rely on non-clean or non-renewable energy sources, they are literally stealing from future generations. This is not a political statement. It is a common-sense truth that leaders of business-owning families have long known and understood. Having this thinking innate to their decision-making is a resource, a highly valuable one that has contributed to their sustainment of competitive advantage. Thankfully, those outside the family business domain have caught on. While this issue may still be at the whim of regulators and political dynamics, it is not negotiable for long-term-oriented business-owning families and their stakeholders. This attitude is one of the values that has been converted into value over time. The return on maintaining this philosophy is ongoing.

Familial Meta-Framework: Philanthropy Leader

One of the pathways included in the big tent framework is that the of leader of philanthropy. The thinking behind the big tent, recall, is that it is preferred that family members are "inside the tent," where opportunities can be created to contribute in a meaningful way. More specifically, individuals will be given the resources to ensure they are ready, willing, and capable to contribute. A role as a leader of philanthropic initiatives is a key route to contribution. Philanthropy is one of the activities among the many that manager–stewards must manage on behalf of owners. To do this requires a strategic approach, with transparency and accountability. This strategic approach, further, will ensure that decisions made to pursue initiatives related to the natural environment are aligned with the values of the business.

Given that philanthropy leaders often occupy a world in contrast to the circumstances of their siblings or cousins in family business commercial activities, these people can also act as the family's appointed "conscience" for how best to optimize environment-related opportunities.

Individual Meta-Framework: Organizational Stewardship

We discussed the servant leadership dimension of organizational stewardship above in the section on social perspective. Here's what happens when it is repositioned to focus more intentionally on the natural environment: organizational stewardship now describes the extent to which leaders prepare an organization to make a positive contribution to society through their commitment to environmental preservation. Organizational stewardship involves an ethic or value for taking responsibility for the environment, ensuring that the strategies and decisions undertaken reflect the commitment to leave the world better than one found it. Servant leaders also work to develop a community spirit that promotes, with a sense of urgency, the importance of the natural environment as a stakeholder when considering all decisions. The servant leader's positive legacy correlates directly with how they champion the need to link environment-focused attitudes to continuity.

The overarching message here is that contextualizing the themes in the various dimensions enables a richness and texture that would otherwise be missed. This approach broadens and deepens the messages inherent in the dimensions and is one that skilled continuity modelers embrace. A related message is that there is often no need to look further than the existing frameworks for ways to tell your story. The stress-tested, theory-driven, evidence-based frameworks are both robust and malleable. Use them idiosyncratically to create your nuanced narrative.

Generational Meta-Framework: Learn to Lead

The third L in the four Ls framework is about embracing the opportunity to co-lead. In the study from which the framework is developed, the leaders examined were found to have perspicacity. Admittedly, for a long time I did not understand the importance of this, but I've come to observe this characteristic in the leaders I have had the honor to get to know. What it means is that they have *insight*: into the business, into the family, and into themselves. Taking this one step further to embed this into the natural environment, it is possible to suggest that this innate *and* learned (yes, not either–or, but both) insight enables them to appreciate the importance of environmental preservation to their family, along with their business's success, growth, and sustainability.

The insight into themselves is important to clarify. My interpretation of this is that in cases when they are not naturally going to be card-carrying Greenpeace™ environmental warriors, they know they don't have to be. Still, they have the insight to know they need to embrace environmental custodianship if they have any chance of handing over commercial activities to future generations. This insight helps them understand it's not about *either* concentrating on preserving the environment or their business but is their responsibility to *both* preserve the environment and grow the business.

Tactical Meta-Framework: Innovation and Learning

The innovation and learning perspective of the balanced scorecard makes it possible to track the intentional inclusion of the natural environment into operations. As highlighted earlier, this will ensure that metrics are established and managed. This also means that those throughout the organization will pay more than lip service to environmental matters.

Integrating environmental preservation solutions into innovation agendas boosts potential to embrace continuing differently. It also has the added benefit of being relevant to a new generation of employees, customers, and suppliers. Business-owning families who understand this protect the environment because it is the right thing to do, rather than merely to comply with some regulatory directive. That is the distinction that needs to be reinforced, as it is part of what got you this far and what will help enable you to continue competitively.

Fundamental Meta-Framework: Technology Development Capability

Technology development capability, one of the four capabilities in the innovation capabilities framework, underlies measuring environment-preservation initiatives and output through the balanced scorecard. In this context, development capability is concerned with how new products and/or processes reflect current and future attitudes toward the natural environment. Technology development is more than technological change, as the primary goal is to provide innovative solutions to the market. Linking this with the innovation and learning paragraph above, it is noteworthy that one of the defining aspects of the balanced scorecard is the focus on tracking lead indicators. The message here, in innovation and learning as well as in innovation capabilities parlance, is the need to focus resources (talent, finances, and others) on developing and bringing to market products and processes that will pass any test of environmental "friendliness." Everyone – yes, everyone – must be vested and vigilant in this regard, or risk being yesterday's story, rather than tomorrow's.

Talent Perspective

- **Objective:** To develop our people.
- **Measures:** Employer of choice survey; percent promoted from within; retention rates; and funds committed to education.
- **Targets:** Improve year on year; and 70% promoted from current workforce.

Keystone Meta-Framework: Principal Cost

Those interested can keep in mind that the principal cost theory was generated by law scholars (but no need to focus on that in depth here). The takeaway, when used for our purpose, is around the need to control costs through the awareness of conflict and competence in principals and, given that in Part I we suggest that principal–agent dyads exist organization-wide, this becomes a relatively easy story to tell when looking at talent across the board.

Recall, at the top of the organization, the principal was the owner, and the board was the agent; then the board was the principal, and the CEO was their agent; then the CEO was the principal, and the top management team was their agent. The top management team members, in turn, become the principal in the dyadic relationship between them and their line employees. So, given that the stated objective in this perspective is "to develop our people," a key imperative would be to concentrate on their being competent to do their tasks, and this holds throughout the organization. It also holds, obviously, for family members not involved in the business, as will be covered in detail in Talent: Successors' Talent Development Planning for Continuity.

Familial Meta-Framework: Community

The Millers' study highlighted the role of people in business families to contribute to longstanding success. They used powerful phrases such as "uniting and tending to the tribe" (2005a, p. 38); "to cherish the firm meant to treasure those who staff and sustain it" (2005b, p. 521); "stratospheric" levels of loyalty and motivation characteristic of the cohesive internal community (2005b, p. 522); "cohesive, gung-ho community of employees" (2005a, p. 38); and "enlist employees in the good fight; and an informal way of operating that engages interaction and collaboration" (2005a, p. 39). The researchers highlight the development of a community of employees charged with nurturing the "precious enterprise and striv[ing] to achieve its hallowed mission" (2005a, p. 42), by working with and on behalf of the family; these stakeholders succeed together by displaying a "moral commitment to enter into an enduring relationship of broad reciprocity – like friendship or even kinship. . .a felt bond between employee and employer" (2005a, p. 42). It is difficult to argue with this: and impossible to say it better than the Millers do.

Individual Meta-Framework: Four Tests Framework

Though not written for this purpose, the four tests framework relates directly to the endeavor of developing people. Recall, the specific types of tests are qualified, self-imposed, circumstantial, and political. The context, as alluded to in the title of the original article, was next-generation leaders of business-owning families. The work emphasizes that testing is ongoing across individual career spans. Taking a broader view, yet again, we can see the tests as a strategic way of planning a career. If it is understood that an independent objective evaluator will periodically use the four tests to assess a person's suitability for a role, it would behoove that person to prepare for that inevitability. This really is a powerful tool, with considerably more application than was likely intended. Integrating this approach into the strategic planning for continuity, moreover, means not having to reinvent the wheel.

Generational Meta-Framework: Learn Business, Learn Our Family Business

Again, the richness of the four Ls framework facilitates its extension to conversations beyond those of business-owning families. Recall that, the study in question here was based on learning and life cycle theories. For the purposes of preparing people, consider the benefit of their having a sound basic understanding of business. While this seems a minimal, no-brainer kind of requirement, that's not always the case. For example, those with technical or engineering qualifications may not have had exposure to a business curriculum. Facilitating this additional education may enhance significantly their understanding of the business to which they have committed their expertise. But regardless, the real benefit is ensuring that the vested community of people is exposed to the opportunity to "learn our family business" (L2). I will not repeat again the single sentence that I recommend you learn by heart. But it is as relevant to non-family enterprise members as it is to family.

My past work with a family in Japan highlighted the importance of the four Ls. Family members immediately bought in to the framework, as most owning families do. But they noted how beneficial it was for planning with their employees and executives, as well. They identified that many of their non-family leaders were stuck in the third L (learn to lead the business) and were, deliberately or otherwise, neglecting to prepare their successors. These leaders had gone to great lengths to recruit the best and brightest graduates but were in denial of the reality that retaining this talent depended on developing the rising cohort for enriching future leadership roles. When this became apparent to all, members of the top management team, who had become much more willing to admit their reluctance about succession, were required to groom more than one successor. Ultimately, the enterprise avoided a sense of panic, which would have resulted had all top executives continued to avoid succession or opted to exit the business together. Instead, everyone felt a new sense of urgency about creating effective successor plans.

The message here is that the four Ls represents a career trajectory map that enables a quick snapshot of the current and future talent situation. Too many people rushing into L3 is problematic, as is an insufficient number transitioning into L4. Instead, spending as much time in L2 is the preferred option, along with co-leading with the incumbents in L3. Stakeholders in general are very interested in how this process is orchestrated. By that I don't mean just those in the operational or executive positions in question, but other vested parties including financiers, customers, and suppliers. Having a talent development planning process, the fourth leg of the scorecard stool, is arguably more important today than ever. It certainly needs to be high on the continuity model planning agenda list, which is why it appears here in the strategic planning process for continuity conversation, as well as represented as a standalone planning process, specifically to develop Successors' Talent.

Tactical Meta-Framework: Four Rs Framework

The four Rs framework complements well the other approaches in this section. It is an efficient, effective way to establish the roles and their attendant requirements, responsibilities, and remuneration. Like the others, this framework's benefits and application extend well beyond the family conversation. Populating the four Rs matrix reduces conflict by making the assumed apparent. This is important for non-family employees, executives, and governors as they consider joining the enterprise in some capacity. Knowing that the four Rs represents a protocol that delineates roles and responsibilities goes a long way in allaying their fears about the characteristic problems that face business-owning families who avoid this level of articulation. If talent is sufficiently important to allocate it as a perspective in the quadruple-bottom-line approach to strategic planning for continuity, simple but effective frameworks such as the four Rs should be interpreted for purpose. If recruiting relies on convincing a candidate that an intentional focus on role clarity mitigates many of the common pitfalls of family business, they will likely welcome and appreciate the many benefits of development of, and commitment to, the four Rs.

Fundamental Meta-Framework: Four Trust Dimensions Framework, Business-Driven Capabilities

Trust impacts everything. Consider the four trust dimensions, discussed in Part I, when evaluating talent: integrity, ability, benevolence, and consistency. The preferred situation is to have all four of these dimensions equally apparent in an individual. If any of the four is compromised, cracks will appear, and trust will be eroded. I highly recommend becoming a student of trust and how it manifests. In this context, the simple four-dimension rubric is necessary but certainly not sufficient to understand trust-based individual and group behavior. But it is a starting point. For example, if the concept of ability is broadened to *cap*ability, the conversation is more relevant to developing people. What this means, most simply, is that an individual is able to do something broad but capable of doing multiple specific tasks. This sits well with the idea of talent development. I also recommend expanding what it means to be benevolent. The trust-related concepts, especially this one, have close associations with servant leadership dimensions, and interested folks should consider how these relate.

You can further foster talent development by integrating a second fundamental meta-frame concept, specifically the business-driven capabilities that are part of the four innovation capabilities framework. So as to not confuse, these can be interpreted by reviewing how I presented them in Part I, which I summarize here. *Management capability* is more general in focus than operations capability. In increasingly complex and unpredictable environments, where problem-solving and decisions rely more than ever on imperfect information, management capability requires a repertoire of skills applied flexibly, including innovative responses to reduce costs that result from uncertainty. *Transaction capability* facilitates the sale of the product or service. Firms that innovate transaction capability gain an advantage because the new products created through technology capability, produced efficiently through processes introduced in operations capability, in an organization where all areas are fine-tuned and run smoothly by capable management, will be transacted economically because marketing, bargaining, and delivery costs are reduced.

What this means is that developing talent for continuity could be interpreted to mean that individuals are encouraged to build both their management and their transacting capabilities. No matter the position, there is an expectation that responsibility is not left to others who have "manager" titles, and that everyone in the organization is responsible for transacting, not just those in formal sales positions.

Put another way, continuity modeling encourages a situation in which you can still be a good manager without being in management, and you can still be a consummate, committed sales ambassador without belonging to the sales department.

Talent: Successors' Talent Development Planning for Continuity

Cornerstone Concept: Develop an Informed Individual Philosophy of Stewardship.

Preamble: Preparing the right people the right way takes careful planning and requires pivoting, in most cases. The end game is a talent pool of all-rounders with complementary skill sets and mindsets to tackle increasingly complex environments. But, just as environments are increasingly complex, so too, it seems, are individuals.

Of the four essential plans for continuity that make up the Continuity Canvas, the successors' talent development plan is arguably the most undervalued. Continuity modeling involves taking a much more expansive approach to planning. This is the most important differentiation between the continuity and succession plan generations. Recall from the strategy planning section that the approach is to extend the process to *all* activities, not just to those associated with the operating entity. Likewise, the asset, wealth, and estate planning process is intentionally expansive. In a similar vein, the successors' talent development planning process looks to nurture individual talent across the individual life cycle and could extend to include accommodating senior generations as they exit full-time engagement in operational roles.

The mantra introduced in the big tent framework is apt and worth revisiting. That is, the aim is to prepare individuals to be ready, willing, and capable to contribute in meaningful ways. Recall that capability, not ability, is preferred, which means that the intention is to build a portfolio of skill sets. Continuity modeling requires a group of skilled individuals with a similar, longer-term horizon mindset. This needs to begin early.

The emphasis put on talent development is a key distinction between the *Continuity Model Generation* and the previous succession plan approach. Put another way, the continuity generation are focused on *successor* planning rather than *succession* planning. A subtle but significant difference.

To assist in the framing of this section, and to help defray what can be a loaded topic, consider the 15 guidelines and pathways that were included in a successor development paper I co-wrote with Ward from his work and others at his consulting group, the Family Business Consulting Group. Succession is inevitable. Even so, it can be the most painful and critical time for family businesses, regardless of their country or culture. Evidence suggests that, globally, less than one-third of family businesses survive into the second generation, and only about 13% make it into the third generation.

After working with hundreds of family businesses on all continents we suggest that there is one underlying, and simple, reason why business families do not handle succession very well, i.e. ***they don't do it very often***. While the tenure of a public company leader is typically between 3 and 7 years, family business leaders lead for 20 to 25 years. In many family businesses, given the change in the commercial landscape over the past two decades, the majority of leaders has never witnessed, or experienced, business succession. In this essay we offer 15 guidelines that we hope will help leaders of family businesses, their families, and those that work with and for them in various capacities, during their impending succession. For each of the 15 guidelines, we include a suggested pathway that either the incumbent leader or the next generation member could (or should) consider, depending on their nuanced circumstance.

1. Succession is a process: *not an event.*

Rather than thinking of succession as an event that happens on a designated day, we counsel to consider thinking of it as a process that occurs over a long period of time. Parents lay the groundwork for succession while their children are still small. How? By the way in which they talk about the business at home.

As the classic story goes, the business owner comes home from a typical day at the shop and shares his or her frustrations related to non-performing employees, a difficult customer, a supplier that has not delivered as promised, and/or an increasingly demanding financier. Then, he or she turns to his son or daughter and says, *"Someday, this will all be yours."* Of course, the truth of the matter is that most people who are in business for themselves love it, or they wouldn't be doing it. However, the tendency is to talk more about the bad events than the good ones. Making a conscious effort to present a balanced perspective on the family business can help the next generation gain a better understanding and appreciation for the business.

Pathway: Ensure that potential successors appreciate there are challenges. . .but that the business also provides some precious opportunities.

2. Present the business as an option: *not an obligation*.

Many parents hope that their children will want to follow in their footsteps and join the family business. But some fall into the trap of over-selling the need to follow the family tradition. Others never bring up the subject because they don't want to pressure their children. The key is to present a role in the business as an opportunity, not as an obligation. How? Parents who seem to do it well explain to their young adult children:

> *Whatever you choose to do with your life, we will support, and we will encourage you. It's probably too soon for you to know now what you want to do. If you should be interested in the family business, you will be very welcome. We have found it to be very rewarding and very fulfilling, but it's clearly not the easiest way to live or the only way to live. It's one of your many options. We will support and encourage you no matter what you decide.*

It is very important to extend a non-conditional offer of support to young adults because it is very healthy for the son or daughter to think in terms of options.

Pathway: Signal consistently that a role in the business is AN option, NOT THE ONLY option.

3. Get outside experience.

ALL of the members of family business that we know who have had the opportunity to get outside experience say that they recommend it highly.

Why should a child work for someone else after finishing their formal education? There are many good reasons why the outside work experience is an advantage. Members of the next generation can build their own identity, get outside knowledge, increase their self-confidence, bring back knowledge to the business, grow up a little bit, make mistakes on someone else's time (and money!) find out what it is like to look for a job, secure the job and get promoted, discover what their market value is, and learn how to be accountable as well as take criticism. But the best reason is that this is how they will learn that the grass isn't greener on the other side of the fence. They will learn that there is no such thing as a perfect boss or a perfect business.

But what if that isn't possible? What if the daughter is 32 years old and is now vice-president of marketing? Or, what if the business is small and they need a family member on sweat equity just to survive? Then, try to find other ways for that son or daughter to get the same sense of reality and outside perspective. Sometimes that means getting involved with their trade association, with other sons or daughters of another family business, or with a community service group.

For many parents, however, it's hard to believe that their children will want to come back to the business after working somewhere else. But the odds are better than three to one that they will come back, because magnetism to the family business generally increases with age.

Pathway: Introduce a requirement that next generation members work for someone else for three to five years. . .and demonstrate competence in their position by being considered for promotion(s).

4. Hire into an existing job.

It's very important to hire a next generation son or daughter into an existing, meaningful, defined job. Why? Parents will

119

know how much to pay and what to expect. The rest of the organization will know how the family member fits into the company hierarchy and how to treat him or her.

But, often, family businesses hire their children into ill-defined jobs and say:

> *Because you are family, you can do anything that needs to be done around here. I wear a lot of hats and now you do, too.*

An unintended consequence of this is resentment on the part of the rest of the employees and management. Sometimes, employees doubt that the next generation member is qualified to lead the company. Don't set next generation sons or daughters up for failure by giving them an overwhelming but undefined job. Create a situation where progress can be measured.

Pathway: Ensure that family members have clear roles, transparent requirements for that role, responsibilities for the role with someone other than a parent to report to and are remunerated at a level consistent with the role.

5. Encourage the development of complementary skills.

After the next generation has entered the business, encourage the development of skills that are complementary to the current leadership. Why? Incumbent leaders' skills are probably well-ingrained in the business by now. If the parents are super salespeople, then the children are going to need to bring some operations or information system skills to the business. If the parent generation is "make it and invent it," then the next generation is probably going to have to know what the terms "market segmentation" and "break-even analysis" mean.

Is it easy to accept the fact that a child can improve or add to the business? No! Parents have to be very secure people to be open to this type of action from their own child. But consider the alternative: is the business better off having a next generation who brings nothing and can only try to duplicate everything that has been done?

There is a cartoon that shows a son saying, "Dad, sales are up 200 percent, production costs are down, and we're profiled in the newspaper." The father says, "Yes, and your shoelace is untied." It's hard to recognize and praise our children's professional achievements.

Pathway: Intentionally equip the next generation with the appropriate knowledge, skills and abilities. . .as the challenges that they will need to address are different to the ones that the current generation navigated.

6. Teach the foundations.

One of the most valuable things the parent generation can give the next generation is an understanding of the historic, cultural, and strategic foundations of the business. It is very useful for the children to be aware of the firm's underpinnings, of the underlying principles that hold the enterprise together.

Even though the current business leaders have lived the business, they may not be able to take a step back and identify clear strategies. Those doing it are often too close to it all. If that is the case, let the child learn from a key employee who is able to explain *why* and *how* things are done. For example, instead of just showing a son or daughter how to treat customers, the key employee will explain how the customer service policy evolved and what advantages the current policy has.

Pathway: Reinforce family values. . .as family values are the foundation of your competitive advantage.

7. Start with mentors.

When members of the next generation enter the business, they should work for a mentor rather than with the parent. The mentor should be the most valuable, the most loyal, the most secure, and the most long-lasting trusted employee. That person should be the incumbent CEO's alter-ego, the one who does all of the things that the current leader doesn't like to do.

When this arrangement is set up, a conversation with the mentor that goes something like this should occur:

> *I would like Karen to work with you because she can learn a lot from you. But I know what will happen in three to five years. You two will clash. It won't be anybody's fault, it's just inevitable that she will want to do something on her own. The moment that happens, the mentoring relationship will end, and I will move her into the next step of the plan that I have in mind for her.*

It is very important to clarify all of this and set it up right from the start. But beware, as even if it has always been made clear that you intend to keep the business in the family, there may be an employee who believes that he or she is better, and more qualified, and rightfully deserves the opportunity to lead the company. Could it be that the employee may attempt to undermine the successor's efforts? Be aware that this possibility exists. Be clear, keep eyes open, and don't let an unpleasant situation build up. The employee may need to be offered two options: recognize the successor's role or leave the company.

Pathway: Share the burden of the next generation's personal and career development with a trusted other.

8. Designate an area of responsibility.

What is the next step of the plan? Give the son or daughter his or her own area of responsibility. It should be well-defined. It could be a certain department. It could be handling the advertising. It could be doing personnel. As the child gains experience and competency, increase the number of areas of responsibility. By giving pieces of the business, all parties will be working toward a smooth succession. Make sure the next generation members are given profit (not only budget) responsibility at some point. . .as that is what they will be doing when they lead the business.

The model that we encourage when thinking about succession is the track relay race. One runner has the baton, and the other runner has to catch up, take the baton, and continue the race. The business will pass to the next generation much more smoothly if that second generation is running at full speed right next to the current baton holder. It should be an exchange that is almost imperceptible.

Pathway: Intentionally design a developmental career that best prepares the next generation for their leadership role.

9. Develop a rationale.

We have just described the ideal transfer. But what if somebody breaks stride or the conditions change? Lots of things could happen. As a matter of fact, the transfer zone is usually a very painful period. The parent may go through a grieving period as he or she says goodbye to the business. But the son or daughter has pain also. He or she may have the most pain.

Maybe there is a disagreement over money. Maybe it is over power. Maybe the founder or current leader is not entirely convinced that the successor is ready. How do both parties make it through this period?

The incumbent leader and the successor could both benefit from forming a rationale or a statement that says *why* all this is worth it to each of you. When things are particularly painful and individuals are wondering why they are going through this, they can tell themselves, "It's difficult now, but it's worth it because. . ."

For example, after thinking things through, a conclusion may be, "It's worth it because we employ a lot of people, and I'm proud to be part of this business." Sorting out feelings will help though this difficult time.

Pathway: Expect that there will be difficult times. . . and support each other through open and honest communication.

10. Recognize that you are not alone.

We have found that it often helps families to know that they are not alone. All families face the same difficult issues such as "How should we valuate the business?" and "Should the founder keep a title like Chairman of the Board?" Somehow, it helps to know that these issues are difficult for everyone who tries to settle them.

It can also help to know that the way in which family members respond to the issues is fairly predictable. In many cases, mothers are over-protective, and fathers think they are invincible. Rather than blaming your oldest son for being too hard-driving and too achievement-oriented, consider the fact that almost all firstborn children are like that. Rather than blaming the youngest child for not taking the business seriously, consider the fact that the baby of the family is usually light-hearted.

Rather than thinking that family members have "personality problems," recognize that it is very natural for the people involved to feel the way they do.

Because conflicts are universal, it is possible to learn from other people who have gone through them. That's why we generally recommend joining family-business networks. Not only will it facilitate seeing how other people resolve their problems, but individuals will appreciate that they may not be as alone as they had previously thought. There is almost always someone who is in a worse situation.

Pathway: Focus on the outcomes you most value.

11. Have family meetings.

Of course, good communication among the family is essential. Sometimes productive communication occurs spontaneously, and sometimes it needs to be planned for. At a family meeting, all the family gets together to discuss an important matter. Sometimes it is best to hold them at an outside neutral location, like a resort or a restaurant; sometimes it is best to sit around the kitchen table.

There are multiple ways to begin. Some families elect to start by selecting a topic and moderator. We usually recommend, however, that things are kept informal and relaxed so that everyone can participate comfortably. The benefits of these meetings typically include a greater feeling of unity (or team building), a clearer understanding of the issues, and a better understanding of the family's range of perspectives.

Pathway: Communicate and educate. . .Communicate and educate. . .Communicate and educate.

12. Plan, plan, plan.

Long before the succession should take place, the incumbent leader should be encouraged to write a business plan, a personal financial plan, and a succession plan all at once. While this is seemingly asking for the near impossible, we do it anyway because it works. These plans need to be written at the same time because they influence each other.

This is not, however, a do-it-yourself project. Help from trusted advisors (the family accountant or attorney), and someone who has knowledge of organizational development is critical. The task is to bring these experts together and develop the plans that can guide everyone through the succession period.

It will NOT be easy, and it will take time. But the long-range benefits of this approach cannot be overstated.

Pathway: Document business, financial, and succession plans as the first item on your to-do list. . .and recruit trusted others who will ensure you don't procrastinate.

13. Create an advisory board.

We recommend advisory boards to *all* small businesses. Why? It is an extremely valuable sustaining resource. The board should include the type of people mentioned above (lawyer, accountant, and organizational specialist) and at least one other person from your industry who gives you respect. Often, the business owner will offer the board members an honorarium instead of a salary. You will benefit from group discussions of important issues.

Pathway: Recruit caring constructive critics to assist in the process.

14. Set a date.

As early in the process as possible, determine a realistic and financially advisable transition date. When incumbent leaders' plans are complete, a clear picture of the leadership evolution process will appear with the ultimate outcome that the business is ready to be handed over to the next generation. It is essential that the incumbent leader is fully committed to that date, that the organization is aware of the plan, and that the successor can depend on the leader to follow through with it.

We have emphasized many times that succession is a process. Choosing a retirement date, preparing the successor, preparing the business for transition, and preparing current leadership for a different sort of life are all vital components of that process.

Talent: Successors' Talent Development Planning for Continuity

Pathway: Consider succession as a life-stage change and that you are <u>moving to</u> another role with different requirements and responsibilities.

15. Let go.

Why do so many founders or leaders at the end of the transition process say, *"Well, I was wrong. We are not going to be able to complete the transition this year after all"?* Or, even worse, why do so many decide that they want to come back to the business two or three years after they left it for good?

It is hard to let go of responsibility. It is hard to let go of authority. But it is even harder to let go of control.

One of the goals that should be central to writing a business plan, personal financial plan, and succession plan is to create financial security that has no ties to the business. Leaders who are vacating need to be financially independent. . .otherwise it will be very, very difficult to resist the temptation of interfering with the business.

Pathway: Prepare in advance to be financially secure and not a burden on the business and. . .Lead by leaving.

In conclusion, perpetuating a family business is the ultimate management challenge, no matter the constituency. The 15 guidelines and pathways we have included here are distilled from working with families of all sizes and in all industries in most countries. This experience has reinforced to us that families across the world are more the same than different. We are hopeful that family business leaders will consider some, if not all, of these guidelines, and therefore be positioned to continue to make significant positive social and economic impact. . .across generations.

Successors' Talent Development Planning for Continuity I: Collecting and Collating Basic Information

Building the successors' talent development section of the Continuity Canvas first involves collecting and collating descriptions and demographics of members. In other words, a list of "who is who in the zoo." Required are basic facts related to gender, age, education, work experience, and the like. Many families will have progressed on this already and have the relevant information at hand. Typically, though, it won't be updated as it would be if it were part of the duties of a human resources department. When approaching this plan, then, best to think and act like a human resources department would.

Indeed, as it soon becomes apparent, this is HR101 with a family twist. So don't get trapped into reinventing the wheel with this or any other process in building the Continuity Canvas. The processes have been long established, so effectively you're contextualizing them to the family, broadening the scope to a wider range of positions and responsibilities, and extending the time horizon.

Once you collate the basics, it's time to commence an individual development plan, or at least attempting to. This is not a perfect science, but science can be applied. Personality- or traits-based psychometric testing is increasingly employed to establish early-stage career leanings. This may then help to create pathways. Importantly, all individuals need a plan, but these plans will inevitably vary in sophistication and granularity. Again, to reinforce, the distinction between Continuity Modeling and previous approaches pertains to the broader perspective.

Consistent with this, talent development planning extends to the incumbent generation and provides a vehicle to discuss ways that senior family members can continue to contribute meaningfully – that is, without meddling.

The third activity for this plan is coming up with a plan of attack (Illustration 27). Given the heterogeneity of the family system, with the emerging family of families, it's only normal that there will be some initial pushback. Moving from a succession plan mindset to a continuity model mindset requires a more expansive approach and involvement orientation. Some will not be comfortable with the idea: having someone else "plan their lives" could understandably feel like an intrusion. Reinforcing that there are four essential plans that are independent but interdependent should help allay their concerns. Moreover, positioning this as an overall process that will enrich the individual and collective experience and not detract from how people spend their time will also be of benefit. But it's critical to take a collaborative approach to each individual. The doing part of this requires

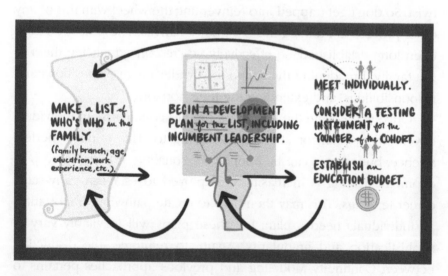

Illustration 27 THREE-STEP APPROACH PLAN FOR THE SUCCESSORS' TALENT DEVELOPMENT PLAN

a process champion and, potentially, a human resource professional. Setting up is the easy part. Maintaining the records is the challenge.

Successors' Talent Development Planning for Continuity II: Cornerstone Concept Equals Develop an Informed Individual Philosophy of Stewardship

With the basic demographic information in hand, the table is set for the second stage, and for the application of selected frameworks to enhance the understanding of requirements to develop a successors' talent development planning process for continuity. The cornerstone concept here is to develop an informed individual philosophy of stewardship. This has two key aspects: (i) individual, and (ii) philosophy of stewardship.

Keeping true to our model here, the overarching objective is to develop a family human resource planning process for continuity that is driven by the 21 frameworks. For this plan, we are concerned with how the frameworks apply to four developmental categories: (i) values, history, and legacy; (ii) financial literacy and value creation; (iii) governance role preparation; and (iv) individual development.

The first task is, again, to consider which of the 21 frameworks will help you populate the 4 developmental categories. The figure below (Illustrated Table 2) provides an example, and summary statements follow to describe the choices and their rationales in more detail. Keep in mind that there are others that could be included to enhance or replace these.

We construct this map by cross-referencing the four development categories with the dimensions that make up the frameworks. Where there is not an obvious matchup, the framework is listed. The intent is twofold: (i) to add breadth and width to the discourse and understanding, (ii) to provide an opportunity to become even more acquainted with the frameworks and appreciate how they apply to the *Continuity Model Generation* and the Continuity Canvas development processes. This is the process to follow to build your own Canvas.

Developing this plan involves, perhaps more than for other plans, taking what can seem like abstract concepts and making them personal.

Values - History - Legacy	Keystone: Stewardship & Resource-based View Familial: Commitment to Us Individual: Altruism Generational: Learn our Family Business (L2) Tactical: The Steward Fundamental: Benevolence
Financial Literacy & Value Creation	Keystone: Economic Familial: Executive/Employee Individual: Self-imposed Test Generational: Affordable Loss Tactical: Financial Perspective of the BSC Fundamental: Renewal
Governance Role Preparation	Keystone: Three Circles Familial: Business/Family Governor Individual: Governor Exit Style Generational: Cousin Consortium Tactical: The Governor Fundamental: Ability and Consistency
Individual Development	Keystone: Three Circles Familial: 4 Ps Individual: Political Test Generational: Learn to Let Go (L4) Tactical: 4Rs Fundamental: Trust Dimensions

Illustrated Table 2 POPULATING THE FOUR DEVELOPMENT CATEGORIES USING THE FRAMEWORKS

You have full license to do that. Indeed, how I approach this may not be your way, and it is not intended to be prescriptive. Allow the frameworks to talk to you. Use the interpretation below simply as a guide, not a panacea.

Values – History – Legacy

Keystone Meta-Framework: Stewardship and Resource-Based View

The concepts of stewardship theory are divided into individual and organizational dimensions, each with three subdimensions. Originally introduced within the management literature, the theory was later contextualized to family-owned businesses. But the concepts have deep roots in the psychology literature, and going back to that core is enriching, particularly for the individual aspects of these Continuity Canvas plans. In this context, overlaying your interpretation of the previous generation's stewardship behavior on your own can be a useful exercise. For example, though you have no doubt heard ad nauseum what your forebears did that was so "amazing," take the time to think about these narratives using the individual aspects of stewardship. Think about their motivation, what drove them to succeed. It was more likely that which drove them to *survive*. This would certainly point you to understanding that their motivation was intrinsic rather than extrinsic. Then, revisit some of the stories about their "leadership" style. You have probably heard the stories a thousand times and read the family and business annals, but think about how they almost definitely saw the business as an extension of themselves. And how do you think they used power? More than likely, they did not emphasize positional power, but wielded personal power. Then, contemplate how you want to be remembered by comparing these deep-rooted behaviors with your own. This critical exercise moves you closer to the cornerstone objective of this planning for continuity process, which is developing your own philosophy of stewardship.

Parallel this line of thinking with understanding that the values that are embedded in you, your family, and by extension your business activities, are resources that are valuable and hard to imitate. By taking stock of these familial resources, you will truly be able to appreciate your forebear's legacy.

Familial Meta-Framework: A Commitment to Us

Having a commitment to us, to be meaningful, requires an understanding of "us." This is housed in the stories that make up your rich family-in-business narrative. However, "us" for you is not the same as "us" for others, and this must be acknowledged. But it rarely is. Your "us" is different from your cousin's "us" because though, in a third-generation example, your parents may be siblings, they both married someone outside your family. So, attempting to establish with significant granularity a definition of "us" will be a fruitless exercise. But establishing in broader terms what it means to be "us" is a pursuit that best-practice families embrace. Here's the challenge: being too broad is pointless (results in platitudes that could apply to anyone) and being too narrow is meaningless. But it is a conversation that has to happen, and the talent development planning process is a good place for it.

Individual Meta-Framework: Altruism

This is how altruism was defined in the servant leadership framework:

Altruistic calling (altruism) describes a leader's deep-rooted desire to make a positive difference in others' lives. It is a generosity of the spirit consistent with a philanthropic purpose in life. Because the ultimate goal is to serve, leaders high in altruistic calling will put others' interests ahead of their own and will work diligently to meet followers' needs.

A repurposing to understand the history and the legacy that form the foundation for continuity, and your individual philosophy of stewardship, could look like this:

Those who have led our family of families up to this point have done so because of their deep-rooted desire to make a positive difference in others' lives. I am one of many who have benefited from this desire. I am determined that their generosity of spirit lives on through me and, to the extent I can influence, those who follow me. Just as putting others' interests ahead of their own was a signature characteristic of my forebears, this too will guide my behavior and decision-making.

Generational Meta-Framework: Learn our Family Business

So much needs to happen in this second L of the four Ls framework, as has been stressed throughout this book. For the purposes of this dimension of the successors' talent development plan for continuity, whether you are positioning yourself for an operational role in the business doesn't matter. You need to learn your family business. I trust that by now you know the sentence that needs to be known by heart *(learn the value of values, keep the philosophies but not the detail, in order to continue differently)*. So, take the time to interview those who hold the stories. . .again. Why? Because the first hundred times you heard them, you may not have been ready to listen. You will regret not having spent the time with the story-keepers when your grandchildren sometime in the future ask you to talk about *your* grandfather, for example. Do it for your kids' kids.

Tactical Meta-Framework: The Steward

As you should recall, earlier in the book we added the word "steward" to each of the labels for constituents in the three circles framework: family, owner, manager. And I've woven that concept throughout the subsequent narrative. To deepen your understanding of what being a "steward" means, consider that the concept of intrinsic motivation is arguably the key driver of what distinguishes individuals committed to family business continuity. Because it is intangible, intrinsic motivation is hard to define. It comes from within. Moreover, being difficult to define makes it hard to teach. Like many of the frameworks here, it needs to be interpreted. It is not something that can be taught in business school. In sum, if the stated (or implied) intention is to perpetuate, there must be an appreciation of what stewardship means, and that relies on an interpretation of intrinsic motivation.

A second dimension of the individual component of stewardship relates to how those involved identify with the business. In other words, stewards see the business as an extension of themselves. As one sixth-generation family leader shared, "In my experience, those genuinely serious about a role in their family business don't see it as a job, nor a career. . .it is more akin to a vocation." In contrast, another leader on a separate occasion reminded me that "ability is thicker than blood," reinforcing that increasingly complex businesses require well-equipped stewards.

The third dimension relates to how stewards use power. The steward doesn't rely on positional power to engage stakeholders. They use personal power. Titles, further, rarely matter for stewards. A sense of entitlement is the enemy of continuity. Stewards who have forged the path to the present appreciated early that they needed to work harder than their nonfamily colleagues because, unlike the family member steward in many cases, they earned their job.

Fundamental Meta-Framework: Benevolence

All four trust dimensions form the foundation of the historical story, the values, and the subsequent legacy that must be understood as part of successors' talent development. Benevolence correlates strongly with the altruism dimension included earlier in this section. Use benevolence as the key to open the "trust box." Ask yourself this simple question, "What role did benevolence play in my fore-bear's journey?" Using trust to drive your thoughts and curiosity, ask about the role of trust *within* their business, *within* and *between* their family and ownership system, and between and among other stakeholder systems. This stream of inquiry will be highly fruitful. Use trust questions, also, to elicit stories from senior enterprise members. This will add significantly to the way you look at the past. Try it. Include it in your own philosophy of stewardship. Be specific, as it is central to all else.

Financial Literacy and Value Creation

Keystone Meta-Framework: Economic

Living by the notion that "there is a business component to every-thing" is a good way to appreciate the need to plan for a meaningful role in the family business system. The economic dimension of the dual logics framework, moreover, focuses the lens on the need for the business activities to perform well. But there is also an economic perspective in the family activities, one that is often overlooked. One way to understand this is by considering that an executive role in the business requires a C-Suite skill set and an "F-Suite" mindset (family-oriented), while a senior role in the family requires an F-Suite skill set and a C-Suite mindset. I elaborated this thinking in a 2017 *Kellogg Insights* article and share it verbatim here:

In addition to C-Suite capabilities such as development of sound business, financial, marketing, and operations strategy and tactics to drive profitable growth, executives need something else as well, something critical: an F-Suite mindset.

Here's what I mean by that. An F-Suite mindset includes the virtues inherent in family businesses: long-term vision, community engagement, a sense of legacy, and clear values. The most effective leaders not only understand these deeply but harness and implement them across every area of the business – from strategy, to hiring, to culture – thus, preserving the founders' vision and values while ensuring that the business can deliver on its mission and strategy.

The two types of skills and mindsets work in tandem in family business: the C-Suite needs to understand the nuances and idiosyncrasies of the family's tradition and values, and the F-Suite must recognize the importance of driving growth. In other words, the same mindset and skill set approach can be applied to those who are not involved in leading the business but assigned leadership roles in the family. You just flip the terms and consider that those in the F-Suite require an F-Suite skill set and a C-Suite mindset. That is, they require the skills to manage familial relationships but need to be aware of the challenges faced by those making the business decisions (related to growth, strategy, and the like).

More specifically, when a family business transitions from the founders to the second generation, it's critical to use the established purpose (typically emphasizing long term over short term), values, and culture of the family or business to inform the development of strategy and tactics going forward, that is, the F-Suite must inform C-Suite decision-making. At the same time, operating well and growing as a second-generation business, typically with larger-scale targets and expectations, requires evolving C-Suite capabilities on top of an F-Suite mindset.

In short, while the skills needed to work at a family firm such as SC Johnson or a nonfamily corporation such as Proctor & Gamble may be similar, the mindset required will be very different, with incorporation of an F-Suite mentality critical for the former.

Moreover, recognizing the importance of the F-Suite and mastering the related mindset will become even more important in managing family businesses in the twenty-first century, as family-owned firms face rising challenges related to business environment factors including competition and customers.

So, what that effectively means is that financial literacy is a prerequisite for roles in the business (en route to the C-Suite) or the family (as part of the F-Suite). As part of that literacy, an understanding of how to create and capture value is useful when orchestrating what needs to be done to develop talent. Having exposure to this helps to contribute to conversations related to present business activities and, perhaps more applicably, to acquisition targets. Regardless of the organizational life cycle stage, understanding how to create and capture value is the purview of all continuity modelers. Recall, the four ways to capture true value are through different types of engineering: specifically, operating engineering, financial engineering, governance engineering, and multiples arbitrage (market timing, multiples expansion). Everyone should acquaint themselves with these.

Familial Meta-Framework: Big Tent Executive or Employee

The big tent framework is all about pathways to contribute meaningfully. A prerequisite for involvement as an executive or an employee is financial literacy. Here, this refers to the idea that you are an executive or employee of the assets that you currently own or will own in the future. If so, there is no point in avoiding the fundamentals of finance. I often hear family business members share that they do not understand "the numbers." That's a myopic view. A simple start is appreciating that financial competency does not have to be at CPA level. Everyone needs to know the basics. The reason is that, ultimately, they will move up the ownership totem pole and should be prepared as early as possible for associated responsibility. In short, avoid understanding the basic financial indicators and dynamics at your peril. It just doesn't make sense if you are managing a considerable portfolio of assets and investments that you would not take the time to make sure they are fundamentally healthy. In fact, treat this priority with the same care as you do for your own health. It is that important.

Individual Meta-Framework: Self-Imposed Test

The four tests framework reinforces the need to develop financial competency. The thinking here, again, is that at some point in time an independent, objective evaluator will be asked to establish whether you have the all-round capacity to perform a particular role. The specific role doesn't matter. What matters is that this process will uncover your Achilles heel, assuming you have one. Put another way, if financial understanding has been something that you have been able to avoid, intentionally or circumstantially, there will come a time when this counts against you. The thinking behind the four tests is the idea of taking a proactive, strategic approach to your career development. The example of the need to address a shortcoming related to financial literacy is a strong application of this framework's richness. Developing the skills proactively will negate future disappointment. This is equally applicable to those who may have the requisite financial skills but lack other capabilities such as management or marketing or logistics. Arrange to secure at least a minimal understanding, because this self-imposed effort will pay dividends. And by dividends, I mean broadly that this will facilitate an increase in confidence and preparedness to contribute meaningfully to the stated goal of continuity.

This is as a good a place as any to further introduce the need to understand how to create and capture value. Recall in an earlier section (see, the decline dimension of the five-stage life cycle framework in the fundamental meta-framework) four ways to capture value were tabled. These were through different types of engineering, specifically operating engineering, financial engineering, governance engineering, and multiples arbitrage (market timing; multiples expansion). This is important to know for anyone involved in the business, no matter their role, and deserves elaboration. The easiest way to make this real is to give the example of when a decision is being made whether to acquire another business. Having an appreciation of how value can be captured (i.e. either through operations, financial restructuring, addressing governance shortcomings, timing the purchase, or a combination of one or more of these) is a fundamental insight everyone involved with the decision should possess.

This understanding is necessary but not sufficient. As individuals evolve up the ownership totem pole, they will need to evolve their understanding of finance. This sounds more daunting than it actually is. Here is my attempt at capturing the basics of finance in one short paragraph, which should hopefully motivate readers to embrace becoming more familiar with what is, and for some has been, previously a no-go zone.

Value is created through the generation of future cash flows at rates of return that exceed the cost of the invested capital. In other words, the combination of growth and return on invested capital (ROIC) drives value and value creation. A corollary to this is that anything that doesn't increase cash flow via improving revenues or returns on capital doesn't create value. Another cornerstone suggests that the value of a business depends on who is managing it and what strategy they pursue.

Generational Meta-Framework: Affordable Loss

The applicability of Sarasvathy's effectual reasoning approach is understanding how entrepreneurs' thinking and behavior has relevance to the need to take a broader view to financial fundamentals. Taken literally, affordable loss relates to not being overly focused on how much will be made but rather to emphasize what can comfortably be lost. Taking a broader perspective, the message could be interpreted as the need to be consistently conscious of what you are prepared to risk. At stake in continuity terms is the long-term health of the business and family. Knowing that taking managed risks is fundamental to financial success, the ability to balance risk and return is requisite. What you can afford to lose, or what is at stake, as it relates to individual investment decisions and how these collectively impact the bigger picture is something you must carefully consider.

An example of this may be when turbulent financial times happen – and they will – and more capital is required to bolster balance sheets, so there could be a movement to sell some assets. Yet, some of these target assets have meaning beyond their book value. They may have sentimental and historical value far beyond what they would fetch in the market. This then becomes a part of discussions around how to quarantine assets and do some scenario planning about risk, with the full understanding of what you can afford to lose. While this may seem abstract in thinking terms, it is a good example of how these frameworks could and should be used. Exercises like this one yield broadened and deepened thought. Commit to them. It is required to construct your Continuity Canvas. If it were easy, I would simply offer a how-to book and let you color it in. It isn't that simple.

Tactical Meta-Framework: Financial Perspective of the Balanced Scorecard

The balanced scorecard, or BSC, framework shows up repeatedly in this book for a reason. This excerpt of a publication I co-wrote with Moores (*Handbook of Research on Family Business* 2006, p. 198) helps bring to light the role of financial perspective as a lag (or lagging) indicator and how this needs to be complemented by the other lead indicators. We also discuss tangible and intangible indicators:

> *Originally developed as a performance measurement tool (Kaplan and Norton, 1992), the BSC has evolved into an organizing framework, an operating system, and a strategic management system (Kaplan and Norton, 1996). As exclusive reliance on financial measures in a management system is insufficient, the BSC highlights the difference between lag indicators versus lead indicators. Financial measures are 'lag indicators that report on the outcomes from past actions' (Kaplan and Norton, 2001, p. 18). Examples of lag indicators are return on investment, revenue growth, customer retention costs, new product revenue, revenue per employee, and the like. These lagging outcome indicators need to be complemented (supplemented) by measures of the drivers of future financial performance, that is, lead indicators.*

Examples of lead indicators are revenue mix, depth of relationships with key stakeholders, customer satisfaction, new product development, diversification preparedness and contractual arrangements.

The BSC also addresses the measurement and management of tangible versus intangible assets. Examples of tangible assets include items such as inventory, property, plant, and equipment (Chandler, 1990) while examples of intangible assets are 'customer relationships, innovative products and services, high-quality and responsive operating processes, skills and knowledge of the workforce, the information technology that supports the workforce and links the firm to its customers and suppliers, and the organizational climate that encourages innovative problem-solving and improvement.'

(Kaplan and Norton, 2001, p. 88).

Fundamental Meta-Framework: Renewal

I include the life cycle stage of renewal here as a reminder that continuity is dependent on the ability to renew. Indeed, complacency is another enemy of continuity modelers. An innate restlessness is required to constantly question business models. This restlessness involves continuous probing to challenge the status quo. Broadening financial metrics from the typically accepted is one way to do this. This involves being prepared to make brave decisions (revisit the command dimension of the four Cs).

Those who study dynamic capabilities share important perspectives related to renewal. They suggest that leaders need to "eat their business model" at times. More specifically, transformation and renewal happen more regularly today than at any time in history. Anticipating change, challenging current beliefs and mindsets, seeking to understand patterns from multiple data points, making (asset-light) commitments with incomplete information, ensuring tough issues are surfaced to pinpoint misalignment, and staying agile and able to course-correct quickly if off-track represent more than a leadership or management responsibility. They are fundamental to hope of continuing. These are the sorts of bullet-point commitments and reminders that continuity modelers make for themselves and ensure in others, no matter their role in the business. Build this into your philosophy of stewardship. It is meaningful. . .and powerful.

Governance Role Preparation

Keystone Meta-Framework: Three Circles

Each of the three circles – family, owners, managers – must be governed. This is the focal subject of one of the other plans here. However, governance role preparation is included as a perspective for successors' talent development planning for continuity because governance roles will likely become increasingly prominent as the business evolves and the family grows. Stipulating that an integral part of developing successors' talent is preparing individuals as governors signals that an operations role in the business is an option, but not the only one (think big tent). Families that get that message right, signal that it is eventually likely that individuals will continue as governing owners. That comes with a whole suite of challenges that we will discuss in Governance Planning for Continuity.

Familial Meta-Framework: Business or Family Governor

The big tent encourages meaningful engagement through pathways that ensure individuals are ready, willing, and capable to contribute. If you are genuinely committed to continuity, you should never tire of repeating this line.

When an offspring declares they are not remotely interested in joining the family business – as many will – that should not be a cause for concern if the big tent framework is in play. A parent who has planned for this, will refer to the mantra and reply, "An operations role in the family business has always been an option for you, but certainly not the only one. It has suited me, and suited your grandparent, but we understand your desire to pursue your own dream. However, there are other meaningful ways for you to contribute to the continuation of this proud family legacy. This could be either as a business governor or a family governor. I encourage you to consider these when the time comes. There are initiatives in place that will prepare you for these roles. Thanks for being honest with me."

Enough said!

Individual Meta-Framework: Governor Exit Style

Learning to let go is hard. Exiting to a role as a governor may be a way to reduce the burden of departing a significant leadership role *in* the business. In these instances, titles typically matter. For many, it didn't really matter when they occupied the CEO or Managing Director position, because everyone was aware of their prominence. However, stepping away from such a prominent role may require retitling. This is not abnormal and should be encouraged. Many is the time when a stated "titles have never mattered" philosophy gives way to "I'd still expect to be Chairperson. . .or non-executive Chairperson. . .or. . ." The options are many and should be discussed thoroughly.

In short, having meaningful roles matters, no matter your life stage. Tokenism will only lead to frustration, and even sabotage. That's because busy people need to be kept busy doing something, or they will meddle. Again, not an abnormal problem but a problem just the same. As a solution, one leader titled himself Emeritus

Chairman and G3 Mentor and was charged by the Board, which included family and independent directors, to develop and implement a mentorship program for his 11 grandchildren. He submitted a proposal and was allocated funding. It has been a delight for me to witness this initiative unfold. The mentees are given clear guidelines of their expectations, and the mentor is making real, ongoing meaningful contributions to the family and the business.

The key idea here is to interpret broadly what it means to be prepared to govern. Innovation in governance distinguishes a business-owning family that is prepared for continuity from one that is rule-constrained and not prepared to design structures to fit with their "personality" and situation. Some people make governance more complicated than it should be. . .and that approach will likely deter rather than encourage engagement and participation. And note that this refers to more than just the *Continuity Model Generation!*

Generational Meta-Framework: Cousin Consortium

The four ownership stages signify the evolution of families in business from founder–owner, to single-successor owner or sibling partnership, to cousin consortium. This depiction highlights that radical change occurs twice: once between the founder–owner and the sibling partners, and again between sibling partners and the cousin-consortium owners. Incremental change occurs if the founder–owner transitions ownership to a single-owner successor, and also as the cousin consortium matures and evolves to subsequent generations. Best practice indicates that the sibling-partner owners understand that they need different structures and systems than those that were suitable for their parents and that the sibling partners also appreciate that what suits them is not going to suit their offspring's consortium. Understanding this simple but predictable trajectory is useful in proactively preparing individuals for governance roles. Ideally, once the sibling partners have honed their governance roles and skill sets and see the benefits of the accountability and transparency that good governance brings, they will work collaboratively with advisors and members of the cousin consortium to develop the new model. Think "put in place the protocols before they are needed" from the four Ps framework. The message here, the good news, is that if they get it right, there will be ongoing incremental change as people are rotated into the multiple governance positions established to govern the family, the business, the ownership, and the foundation. More on that in Governance: Governance Planning for Continuity.

Tactical Meta-Framework: The Governor

I captured the sentiments pertinent to what it means to be a governor in the book I co-wrote with Ken Moores that introduced the thinking behind the heterogeneity frameworks. A revisit to this content yielded the following items that anyone preparing for a governance role should consider:

- To govern competently requires a genuine understanding of what it is you are governing and for whom.

- You need to consider yourself concurrently responsible for governing two critical things: your forebears' legacy and your offspring's destiny.

- Making decisions as a governor calls for a different modus operandi than that of being a manager of the business. The mindset and skills required are different.

- Decisions are made with less-than-perfect information, sometimes far less.

- The best way to make a decision is to first craft a thesis; then spin this around deliberately to create an antithesis and with these both in play synthesize the two alternate viewpoints.

- Being proficient at "artful procrastination" helps.

- Never make a decision before you have to.

- You need to develop a tolerance for ambiguity.

- Decision-making should be collegial.

- A key skill to master for successful governance is the ability to persuade and be persuadable. To persuade requires a fine-tuned capacity to provide a compelling argument that is aligned closely with the agreed-upon strategy and embedded firmly in the values and beliefs of the family. What does "persuadability" require?

- Governing requires a genuine understanding of family values.

- There is no point in attending a board meeting with a closed mind. Remember, judgments are made with less-than-perfect information, and it is best to be open-minded to the prospect that you might be persuaded to support a position quite different from the one you entered with.

Fundamental Meta-Framework: Ability and Consistency

Governance preparation requires that you are trusted. That you have the requisite integrity is not likely to be in question. Similarly, that you are acting with benevolence probably won't be an issue. But the other two trust dimensions may come into focus and, consequently, should drive proactive preparation. First, you will have to demonstrate your *ability*. No rocket science here. Knowing that there is likelihood that your role will morph into a governing owner, best to do what it takes to gain relevant ability (sounds like the big tent meets the four tests meets principal cost theory, doesn't it?). A good plan could be to combine learning through director's courses and practical experience in governance roles outside the family board. Philanthropic boards, school boards, and/or industry boards provide good grounding. So, when the time is right, consider sitting on someone else's board. In general, there are multiple opportunities available to the willing to build governance skills and gain exposure. This is good use of your time, though it may not always seem so. In fact, having experience on and exposure to boards that don't function optimally is of value. Seeing glaring and frustrating governance flaws is a good motivator to get it right when the time comes to take a position on your family, ownership, or business board.

The other trust dimension relates to *consistency*. Observing boards that do not function optimally will likely expose you to a case of mistrust due to poor consistency. Such consistency could relate to the timely production of agendas and minutes, for example, or following a predictable meeting process, or even the construction of the meeting calendar. Perhaps more important than these process issues, the consistency by which decisions are made and how stakeholders' perspectives are considered is likely to challenge trust relationships.

The message is clear: to build governance competency as part of the successors' talent development planning process, do not take shortcuts, which are generally not available on the long road to continuity.

Individual Development

Keystone Meta-Framework: Three Circles

Returning to the three circles now is appropriate. Developing an informed individual philosophy of stewardship will require interpreting this, the most widely accepted framework in family business, to build your own narrative. This is the opportunity to add your voice and make it your own. Adding the word "steward" and broadening depiction of the individual circles, as we did earlier, is a great starting point. But make it even more meaningful by using this to frame your individual statement, to craft a more powerful and impactful story. Your story, when combined with those of others you're teaming with to build the Continuity Canvas, will result in a rich tapestry of perspectives. Broaden your thinking by considering the crazy quilt perspective, where you "collude" with others to design and deliver something unique but useful at the same time.

Familial Meta-Framework: Four Ps

Recall that the four Ps are parenting, familial processes, protocols in place before needed, and sense of purpose. All four have relevance as individuals consider their development. Continuity, remember, is likely to be more about continuing differently and contingent on how individuals develop their own "self." Being reminded, and encouraged, to follow your own dream is sage direction. Following your own dream while concurrently contributing meaningfully is both challenging and rewarding. It's not easy, but not impossible. It requires a plan, one that includes how you see yourself in terms of your role as a parent, family member, and someone with an individual sense of purpose. Weave these aspects into your individual philosophy of stewardship.

Individual Meta-Framework: Political Test

I was once reminded, as I described earlier in this book, that the two most important words in the English language are "help me." The fourth of the four tests dictates that an independent, objective evaluator will be curious to establish how well you perform when it comes to the political test. A role at the intersection of ownership, family, and manager (stewards) is potentially politically charged with emotion, agenda, and other minefields. It would be naïve to think otherwise. As such, becoming politically savvy is required, to contribute optimally.

In general, there will be diverse opinions and perspectives (that is even one of the dimensions!), so be prepared to respond to someone who doesn't necessarily see the world as you do with a simple response, like "I understand my viewpoint, can you *help me* understand yours?" This will promote trust and sharpen your ability to ward off a potentially political storm. It is about being vulnerable. Consensus is the desired outcome. Consensus is reached by ensuring that everyone feels that they have been heard. Developing this understanding is as important, if not more, than any other topics covered above. Overall, committing to continuity depends on individuals who interpret stewardship similarly, not in exactly the same way but similarly. Capture your interpretation of the sentiments shared on these pages in *your* individual philosophy. If you have been intentional, deliberate, and genuinely committed, your collective sentiments will align. If they don't, "Can you help me understand your perspective" is a good place to start.

Generational Meta-Framework: Learn to Let Go

Individual development includes developing across the life cycle. The perspicacity, or insightfulness, that is characteristic of the third L stage, evolves into the prescience required to transition into the fourth L. Moreover, staying too long in L3 will sabotage continuity efforts. Think broadly about the application of agency theory, particularly entrenchment. Recognize that you will ultimately be judged based on how you orchestrated your exit, not on any widget you introduced, any sales figures, or any accolades you won. The one award that matters to continuity model generation members is how well the business, the family, and the ownership group was prepared for continuity. That is what should be woven into a philosophy of stewardship.

Tactical Meta-Framework: Four Rs

The four Rs framework outlines the different roles "on offer" in the family, the business, and the ownership system. Using this simple matrix to plan your individual development plan makes sense. It is also a handy tool to educate others in your close family unit, that is, your offspring and spouse.

Follow the prompts: What are the requirements for the different roles? It is that easy. That practical.

Well, actually, it's not that easy. Populating the matrix is complicated. But the process of populating it helps establish that there are differences of opinions. Not better opinions than yours, not worse. Just different. The four Rs framework assists in your individual development by enabling you to question yourself about why you think like you do and to understand why that is different from how others might think, including those particularly close to you, especially your siblings and your parents.

Fundamental Meta-Framework: Trust Dimensions

The definition of trustworthiness is a willingness to be vulnerable. Understand what this means. It matters that you know. Add this to your to-do list. . .now.

Wealth: Asset, Wealth, and Estate Planning for Continuity

Cornerstone Concept: Produce a Handwritten Individual Legacy Statement

Preamble: Continuing in the best financial shape is the holy grail for family business. Everyone knows that. But many postpone doing anything about it. . .until it is too late. Much of continuity hinges on this plan, arguably the most important of the four plans here.

This plan aims to reduce potential for tension between the owners and the broader family. Of the four plans, this is the most sensitive and the most technical. It is also the one most likely to be shrouded in secrecy. Conspiracy theories abound. Moreover, it is also the one most commonly avoided. Yet the image of the crusty old patriarch dying at his desk and ruling from the grave is not consistent with continuity modeling. The Continuity Generation has a more pragmatic perspective. They recognize that strong financial health and familial harmony significantly enhance chances for continuity. So, rather than avoid asset, wealth, and estate (AWE) planning, they tackle this head-on. In general, the Continuity Generation believes that dealing with difficult, sensitive conversations openly addresses much of the inevitable tension in family business. "There *is* another way" is the *Continuity Model Generation* mantra.

Asset, Wealth and Estate Planning for Continuity I: Collecting and Collating Basic Information

What will likely become obvious in these pages is that building your Continuity Canvas takes some patience and a degree of detective work. It may also require difficult conversations previously considered off-limits. Two hints here: (i) tread lightly, and (ii) be prepared to back off and move on from this plan to one of the others if you find that some simply aren't ready for it. But focusing elsewhere does not mean you have given up at the first sign of resistance. It simply suggests that the aim is to build momentum around continuity (and its close relation, legacy, which is a much easier pill to swallow than "succession," for even the staunchest naysayer).

Proceed by looking at the ownership system. It is often surprising, to even the most seasoned experts, how few owners in multi-generational, business-owning families have intimate knowledge about what they actually own. This is not such a big deal with earlier-stage entities, of course. But the situation changes as businesses and families grow, particularly when there is a liquidity event or a generational change in ownership. Here it is important not to fall into the trap of personality and/or family faction judgment. Remember, the aim is continuity. Sometimes it is best to avoid the trap by staying focused on "technical" issues, and to examine ownership structures and entities, rather than individuals as owners. Avoid potential minefields. The more complex the business activities and the older the family (in generational terms), the more difficult and challenging this undertaking. But that is not an excuse, when the aim is to *understand to continue* by *continuing to understand*. So, acknowledge the complexity but aim to keep it as simple as possible. Recall the analogy of ensuring a ten-year-old can follow the gist. Perhaps create an evidence chart, as if you were a detective solving a case. That way there will be a trail.

Start with the understanding that each entity is 100%-owned by someone and work out who owns what portions of that 100%. Do not focus on what that holding is worth. That really does not matter to this conversation. Moreover, be warned that complex trust structures will send you down rabbit holes. Avoid them where possible. In some cases, such trusts may be a delaying tactic by someone not drinking the continuity Kool-Aid™ or inherited and in place for taxation minimization (not avoidance). Regardless, now is not the time to be unraveling these. Instead, flag the need for a future, healthy discussion about whether these structures are contributing or limiting continuity chances. It could be that the trusts must be dissolved and reformulated, in the name of continuity modeling.

The second activity required to build a Continuity Canvas in the AWE planning process, just as was advised in the Strategic Plan, is to honestly evaluate each owner's preparedness to transition their estate, wealth, and assets (Illustration 28). This scrutiny is difficult but necessary. It really is the "day after you bury or burn me" test, morbid as that may be. It involves owners holding a mirror up to themselves and asking how healthy their assets, wealth, and estate are in terms of contributing to or harming the chances of continuity. A generation ago, this was unthinkable. But the Continuity Generation expects, even demands, to know what cards they are going to end up holding. The incumbent generation should know the cards. After all, they are holding them. To not engage is unfair. . .for all stakeholders. Always has been, always will be.

Message to incumbents: set the next generation(s) up for success; don't make it more difficult than it already is. Okay, I'll step off my soapbox now.

There is no one way to go about this step of AWE planning. It is vital that you (i) uncover the evidence in percentage ownership

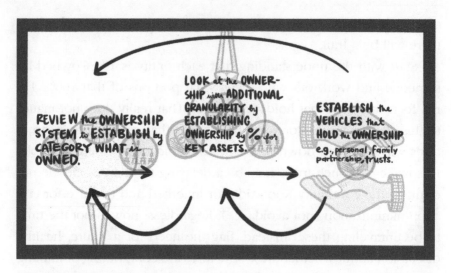

Illustration 28 THREE-STEP APPROACH PLAN FOR THE ASSET, WEALTH, AND ESTATE PLAN

terms rather than dollar figures, and (ii) honestly evaluate how well the wealth, assets, and estate are placed to be efficiently transferred in the future. Consider drafting a table on a whiteboard, and figure it out for yourselves. Likely, you'll eventually require involvement of trusted advisors, lawyers and accountants. But do not outsource the problem to them. It is not their problem. They love problems; indeed, that's their business model.

Tread lightly but do tread into the territories this planning requires.

Asset, Wealth, and Estate Planning for Continuity II: Cornerstone Concept Equals Produce a Handwritten Individual Legacy Statement

As for the previous plans discussed, with some basic descriptive information in hand, the platform is set for the second stage, or the application of selected frameworks to understand more fully what is required to develop an AWE planning process for continuity. The cornerstone objective here is to produce a handwritten individual legacy statement. There are three aspects of this: (i) handwritten, (ii) individual, and (iii) legacy. To clarify, this is not intended to be a legally binding document. It is the opposite. The statement may influence a legal document eventually, but in no way is it intended to replace a will, a trust deed, a whatever. It is the antecedent to many of these documents. It is what it is. . .a hand-written individual legacy statement. More specifically, it articulates one's very personal intentions to be remembered and how any assets, wealth, or estate items can best be deployed or redeployed to raise chances for the business and the family to continue as major contributors to commerce and society. This idea must be stressed and restressed. The ultimate handwritten document, further, contains sentiments typical of a eulogy. Indeed, if it feels more comfortable and helps keep the legal team at bay, call the statement the opening paragraph to your eulogy!

Keeping true to our central model, the overarching objective is to develop an asset, wealth, and estate planning process for continuity that is driven by the 21 frameworks. For this plan, we are concerned with how the frameworks apply to four groups: (i) family–nuclear, (ii) family–extended, (iii) other–individuals, and (iv) other–groups (Illustrated Table 3). Given the personal nature of this activity, it is easier to group the groups and consider more broadly the application of the frameworks. But the intent is to motivate broader and deeper thought processes. It is inevitable that everyone must do this eventually. Doing it as part of the *Continuity Model Generation* process is far preferred to being dragged into a lawyer's office and asked questions for which you are likely not prepared.

Stay in the helicopter. The view (and viewpoint) is better. Avoid getting distracted. Look more through the windshield than at the rear-view mirror. Keep reminding yourself that what you produce is not legally binding; that will come later. It is a commitment to

Family – Nuclear & Extended	Keystone: Owner-steward Familial: Planning is Vital Individual: Altruism Generational: Learn to Let Go (L4) Tactical: The Steward Fundamental: Benevolence
Other – Individuals Groups	Keystone: Social Familial: Communication is Key Individual: Wisdom Generational: Learn to Let Go (L4) Tactical: 4R Fundamental: Trust

Illustrated Table 3 POPULATING THE ASSET, WEALTH, AND ESTATE CATEGORIES USING THE FRAMEWORKS

the understanding that having a plan will significantly reduce tension and the potential for conflict between owner-stewards and the increasingly diverse family of families. If it feels uncomfortable, that is normal and not a bad thing. In fact, embrace the process as being as, or more, important than anything you have done in your career and family life. Keep asking yourself if you are asking the right questions. It doesn't matter what others think if you start to say this aloud. "Am I asking the right questions" is a useful safe harbor to retreat to when you are overwhelmed, no matter the context. You will never get perfect information but knowing that is part of the process of developing a tolerance of ambiguity, which is a prerequisite for continuity thinking. To think and act broadly and deeply about this topic, and plan, really is, as someone once put it, *the final test of greatness*.

Keystone Meta-Framework

I: Owner–Steward: The systems in the three circles framework are not static. Each is in flux. For example, the commercial activities that the manager–stewards manage for the owners are evolving, constantly. The portfolio of assets, the businesses, and the investments change. The overall equity value changes, hopefully positively. Expected returns are at the mercy of many extraneous factors. Some assets are divested. Debts and other borrowings also change. This all has an impact to be acknowledged and monitored.

The owner–steward has a responsibility to carefully consider the implications of their asset, wealth, and estate planning intentions. Having continuity as *the* dominant consideration focuses the owner–steward and informs those influencing their decision-making process.

Dividing beneficiaries, as suggested here, is a non-threatening way for an owner to fulfill their various obligations. It enables them a safe place to begin discussions. One approach is to think of the task in strategic terms as the shared objective. For example, the objective is to ensure that the transfer of wealth enhances family legacy through prudent distribution to family (close and extended), as well as to individuals and groups who have meaningfully impacted your life. This itself could be the start of your handwritten legacy statement.

II: Social: Throughout this book we have discussed the complementary foci of business-owning families. When cascading this to individual AWE planning, it makes sense to acknowledge the social imperatives supported by the business as a collective stakeholder when considering beneficiaries. This can be captured in the other-group category, which also includes individual "pet" projects.

Familial Meta-Framework

I: Planning is Vital: The saying that someone will "die with their boots on and rule from the grave" becomes especially pertinent for AWE planning. The reasons to plan are many, and there's no need for us to list them here. One senior family business owner who had long put off planning his AWE finally found motivation when a confidante

suggested that if he did not act, the lawyers would get the majority of his estate. There is an expectation from the next-generation
that their now-generation commit to approaching this process sens-
ibly. . .by planning.

A revisit to the three circles' diagram you drew in the opening
sections will highlight two major drivers of the need for planning.
One is that the owner–stewards are a heterogenous group. Recall
the economic versus psychological utility we plotted on a continuum. The second is that the family of families becomes larger, more
diverse, and more complicated for multiple reasons.

II: Communication is Key: Those who get it right communicate, communicate, communicate. While many have mastered the
art of difficult business conversations over their careers, having difficult personal or family conversations has not typically been a strong
suit. Avoiding communicating will not make the problem go away.
Though most recognize that truth, they still struggle with it.

When the topic came up in one family, the third-generation successor who had been anointed to lead the business and his generation, asked the second-generation owners – his father, mother, uncle,
and aunt – a simple question: "Can you go away and work out how
much you need?" The second-generation sibling partners had rein-
vested in the business over their working lives. Their reinvestment
had two outcomes. One was that the business had grown considerably, was financially and strategically healthy, and debt-free. The
second was that they did not have sufficient retirement funds to live
comfortably for the following decades. Thus, the successor and his
cousin consortium needed this information about their parents' personal needs so they could develop the financial plan to continue the
growth, and the legacy, while providing sufficiently for the previous
generation.

In another example, a founder wanted to ensure that his second wife was cared for after his passing. But he quickly found that

162

this was not an easy conversation to have with his children, due to some unresolved tension about the second marriage. This is not an unusual occurrence, with ever more "hybrid" families populating the family–steward circle.

The good news is that there are plenty of trusted advisors to facilitate these conversations. That is what they do. Communicate with them early and often. Do not wait for them to have the conversation with you: shock them by bringing it up. That's what a continuity modeler would do. This conversation also needs to happen at the board level. . .with all boards. The discussion falls under the category of "risk," because that is what it is. Put it on the agenda. Lead the conversation.

And yes, the topic of pre-nuptials needs to figure into these conversations. Don't avoid that.

Individual Meta-Framework

I: Altruism: Altruism, one of the five servant leadership framework dimensions we discussed, is about a leader's deep-rooted desire to make a positive difference in others' lives. So, in the spirit of encouraging a broadened, deeper interpretation of the dimensions and frameworks, the message related to altruism in the context of AWE planning could be that careful, meaningful AWE planning ensures altruism does not die with the individual. Follow that train of thought and see where it leads. Optimizing these sentiments requires, among other things, wisdom as discussed below.

II: Wisdom: Wisdom in the servant leadership framework, as previously noted, is a combination of awareness of surroundings and anticipation of consequences. When these two characteristics are combined in an individual, the person becomes adept at picking up cues from the environment and understanding their implications. Awareness and consequences are about perspicacity (think L3 of the four Ls), whereby perspicacious individuals have insight into their family, their business, and themselves. Considering thoughtfully the consequences of any AWE plan requires the wisdom that proponents of servant leadership refer to. Consider broadening and deepening that to AWE when crafting a legacy statement.

Generational Meta-Framework

I: Learn to Let Go: The robustness of the four Ls framework has been on display throughout these pages. It has been suggested that L4, letting go, is the most difficult. To emphasize that, I share here an important excerpt from Moores and Barrett of the original study that generated this framework:

Phase 4: Learning To Let Go Our Business

Learning Priority – Prescience

But letting go is a paradoxical kind of leadership problem, because it has to do with planning what needs to happen when the incumbent CEO is no longer there. That is, the CEO is indeed leading, but in order to let go. A further feature of letting go our business is that, contrary to what the words themselves might suggest, letting go is not so much an event as a process of transition. Let us now examine the stages of letting go the business and the factors that influence how incumbent CEOs of family business learn to handle this process.

Broadly speaking, before their maturity, firms will show 'ascending' characteristics, and after it there is a risk that they will show descending characteristics. Ascending firms are dominated by entrepreneurialism. This manifests itself in a "permissive" control ethos in which everything is permitted unless it is expressly forbidden. Function dominates form in matters of organizational structure. Political power rests with marketing

(Continued)

---

and sales. The leader of a firm at this stage needs to facilitate convergent thinking and mobilize the firm's internal change agents. In descending firms, administrative features dominate. The administrative role may become so disproportionate as to encompass rules about trivia that people respect but no longer understand: "administrivism" rules. A bureaucratic control ethos means that everything is forbidden unless expressly permitted, form dominates function in the firm's structure, and political power rests with its finance and accounting functions.

The task of the leader is to facilitate divergent thinking, and to mobilize external agents of change.

Paradox: Leading to Leave

The process of leaving our business makes the succession process appear logical, even if the problem itself is a paradox: "leading in order to let go". However, according to our informants, being a logical process does not make it an easy one. While new leaders can be catalysts for change, factors at the individual and the firm level can make changes messy and difficult, and this is equally true of succession. As a result, sometimes change or succession can be aborted altogether. Equally, the continuing presence of 'retired' CEOs who have not accepted their new status and found a new role will extend the succession process indefinitely and make it still more difficult. CEOs have to deal with the fact that while they had become accustomed to seeing themselves as the leader, they have to become willing outcasts. That is, they must welcome the presence of being displaced by their own anointed heir.

Yet heirs, who are active and already capably involved in the business, perhaps through a long-standing mentoring process, are essential to the continuation of the business. Well before they move into the top position, they need to be perceived as good performers whom others can trust to

(Continued)

(Continued)

lead the business in future. Equally important is that the designated new CEO be seen to be serious about new strategies or management practices he or she plans to introduce and to have the expertise to introduce them. Making sure all this happens in a timely and orderly way is in large measure the task of the incumbent CEO. It means he or she needs to plan for his or her position as the 'anointed one' to become that of the willing outcast.

As a result, learning to let go the family business is yet another aspect of the paradoxical qualities of leading, since it requires the leader to plan for when he or she will no longer be leading. In essence, the task of learning to leave consists in leading in order to let go. The paradox is that where learning the family business in the earlier stages has involved learning, achieving, justifying one's place as the anointed successor, this stage of learning involves the reverse – the anointed leader must place himself or herself in what feels like the position of a voluntary outcast. To add to the difficulty, most of our informants agree it needs to be done early: sometimes not much later than the time the CEO takes over the reins of power. It involves a mental dissociation from the firm that is conscious and deliberate often just when the firm typically needs the most direct and detailed involvement by those running it – typically as it reaches maturity.

Pathway(s): Multiple

The pathways through the paradox of leading to let go, effectively moving from the position of leader to willing outcast, while difficult, nevertheless have some clarity to them. They include planning early for the CEO's retirement, creating management development plans, and making and keeping to a clear plan for the whole process. They also include the CEO adopting a future role in the business that, preferably, resembles an "ambassador" or "governor" relationship with the firm.

(Continued)

(Continued)

> *Learning to deal with succession – letting go the family business – shares an important characteristic with the other phases of learning we have discussed. The problem of leaving the business, like the other paradoxes, cannot be made to disappear. Yet, despite the pattern of increasing management complexity the problem of family business leadership presents, there are some recurring patterns in the ways successful Australian family businesses have tackled leadership tasks. In line with our earlier discoveries, the stage the firm has reached in its business life cycle provides some important insights into these approaches. So, it is time now to summarize some of the approaches that work – to sketch the profiles of successful Australian family businesses whose leaders have demonstrably managed the intrinsic paradoxes of linking family and business. In short, the pathway is simply:*
>
> * *Develop a defined timeline for retirement;*
> * *Create management development systems;*
> * *Stick to the plan.*

II: Learn to Let Go: Reread the previous section. (Then consider reading it again.)

Tactical Meta-Framework

I: The Steward: A steward is someone who identifies with the organization; they see themselves as an intimate part of the business and, therefore, shoulder responsibility for the organization's success. As a result, a steward will feel satisfaction about the firm's successes and disappointment from its failings, and will work hard to overcome organizational obstacles, aligning their own interest with those of the principals. These stewards, moreover, are motivated not by personal recognition or gain; they benefit only when the organization does. Applying this to the AWE planning process would mean that the consequences of any decisions related to the transfer of assets and wealth will be framed around benefiting the organization, or others. *This* is legacy, and the linchpin of continuity.

II: Four Rs–Role: The owner role entails specific requirements and responsibilities. When you populate the four Rs matrix, remember that this role encompasses careful deliberation about how assets, wealth, and estates will be transferred across generations. That would be the kind of broader, deeper thinking required of the Continuity Generation.

Fundamental Meta-Framework

I: Benevolence: Benevolence denotes a desire to do good. Thus, it is critical to establishing a personal legacy statement. No need to invent new words for this; use the ones gifted by the frameworks.

II: Trust: The four trust dimensions framework provided a simple but effective rubric for how trust manifests in relationships. Extending that to the AWE planning conversation, a broader and deeper perspective yields the opportunity to examine different types of trust. This would reveal that the highest degree of trust is identification-based trust, where a collective identity between the trustor and the trustee is so strong that "each party can represent the other's interests with their full confidence" (Dietz and Den Hartog 2006, p. 564; Lewicki and Bunker 1996). For identification-based trust to evolve, the parties must rely on extensive knowledge about one another's behaviors, needs, and preferences, effectively becoming a shared identity (Lewicki and Bunker 1995; Lewicki and Bunker 1996). It is this level of trust that would be expected to evolve between those transferring their AWE and their beneficiaries.

Governance:
Governance Planning for Continuity

Cornerstone Concept: Craft the Family's Governance Philosophy.

Preamble: Governing the growing family group, the heterogeneous ownership group, and the array of operating and investment entities requires planning and oversight. Members of the continuity model generation are *good* governance *zealots*.

The governance plan, for continuity modelers, really is the keystone in the arch of the canvas. As highlighted previously, this generation sees communication, education, accountability, and transparency as vital to any chance for continuity.

Governance Planning for Continuity I: Collecting and Collating Basic information

The first step here is the same as for the other plans: undertaking an honest evaluation. For some, this will involve diligent benchmarking to establish how others govern their family, their business, and their ownership groups. What this process will reveal is that governance is best understood along a continuum anchored at one end with "informal" and the other with "formal." The mantra that most use when journeying along this continuum typically includes anchor comments such as (i) "What works for the current generation won't work for future generations"; (ii) "Let's act with a sense of urgency not a sense of panic"; and (iii) "Beware allowing the pendulum to swing too far in the opposite direction, as that will lead to over-governing." Or as someone interpreted, "Don't hit a nut with a sledgehammer!"

So, the first task is to know what you don't know. In other words, find out how others govern. The key here is to learn from those who are ahead of you in terms of governance planning, implementation, and functioning. In other words, a sibling partnership should be learning from a cousin consortium. A nascent cousin consortium should learn from a more mature governed family. This will illuminate that effective governance requires a relentless focus on process innovation.

Once in the governance planning lane, the second, usually concurrent, task is to establish what needs to be governed. Do not get too worked up over this. Everything is already governed, albeit in many cases, informally (and it works, to a degree). You are aiming to firmly establish structures and processes that, though they can and will need to be tweaked, will stand the test of time.

Next is deciding who is going to govern. A successful continuity model is predicated on looking forward, ensuring that the positions on various boards are always filled by the best qualified (Illustration 29).

While there are large numbers of books, articles, associations, courses, advisors, and experts to assist in creating governance protocols, the continuity model generation genuinely engages in understanding the governance landscape. This is not something they outsource. The constant question they ask, and others ask of them, is "Are we in good hands?" Put another way, can we trust those who are in decision-making roles in our companies and on our boards? This plan, likely, will ultimately dictate whether continuity will occur relatively seamlessly. These "governance ninjas" constantly seek information about how they can innovate to make governance structures stronger. It is not a set-and-forget approach. Like the other plans, a plan for the plan is required.

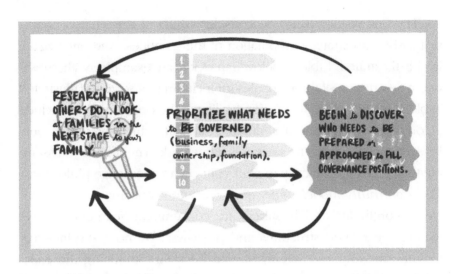

Illustration 29 THREE-STEP APPROACH PLAN FOR THE GOVERNANCE PLAN

The mantra that the continuity model generation lives by goes something like this: The aim of the game is to build trust within, between, and among a team of decision-making teams: within the different boards (business, family, ownership, foundation), between each of these in dyads, (business–family; business–ownership; business–foundation; family–ownership; family–foundation; ownership–foundation), and among the business, family, ownership, and foundation boards.

Governance Planning for Continuity II: Cornerstone Concept Equals Craft the Family's Governance Philosophy

Following the template established in the previous planning processes, the overarching objective is to develop a governance planning process for continuity driven by the 21 frameworks. For this plan, we focus on how they apply to four entities that require governance: (i) the business, (ii) the family, (iii) the owners, and (iv) the foundation.

The first task is, again, to consider which of the 21 frameworks will assist with strategic population of the 4 entities. And once again, in the Illustrated Table 4 below I provide an example, with subsequent description of the rationales for including these items (Illustrated Table 4). Developing this section facilitated the opportunity to include a considerable amount of additional material, which may seem only loosely connected to the assigned framework. The idea is to assemble the pieces strategically to craft your own governance philosophy. The *Continuity Model Generation* considers governance the vehicle of continuity, and members are consummate learners of ways to improve related structures and processes. By now, the message to think broadly and deeply should be clear. Stretching the existing frameworks and complementing these with other concepts and thinking is not only encouraged but necessary.

Governance is a journey. When reviewing the example below, consider for your own situation not just what is needed to govern "the now" but what will be needed going forward; that's critical. Keep in mind that there are other frameworks that could be included to enhance or replace these, to better apply to your business and family life stages. Be cognizant, moreover, that I constructed this example by cross-referencing the four entities with the dimensions that make up the frameworks. Where there is not an obvious match-up, I generally list the framework.

The intent here is twofold. First, to add breadth and depth to the discourse and nurture understanding. Second, it provides an opportunity to become even more acquainted with the frameworks and to appreciate how they can be maneuvered to facilitate different aspects of the continuity model and Continuity Canvas development processes. I intentionally repeat this to stress that this is the process required to build your own canvas.

Business

Keystone: Four Foundational Theories
Familial: Business Governor - Family Governor
Individual: Four Tests Framework
Generational: Learn Our Family Business
Tactical: Governance - The Governor
Fundamental: Renewal - Business-driven Capabilities

Family

Keystone: Family Steward
Familial: Sense of Purpose
Individual: Political
Generational: Learn to Lead
Tactical: 4Rs
Fundamental: Trust

Owners

Keystone: Owner-steward
Familial: 4Ps - Protocols
Individual: Persuasiveness
Generational: Sibling Partnership
Tactical: 4Rs; Responsibility
Fundamental: Church

Foundation

Keystone: Social
Familial: Big Tent - Philanthropy
Individual: Empathy and Altruism
Generational: Crazy Quilt
Tactical: Customer
Fundamental: Business-driven Capabilities

Illustrated Table 4 POPULATING THE FOUR GOVERNANCE CATEGORIES USING THE FRAMEWORKS

Business Governance

Keystone Meta-Framework: Four Foundational Theories

Theorists and other scholars have spent lifetimes trying to figure out governance. The nomenclature has evolved over time, but "corporate governance" seems to be the current agreed-upon positioning. In simple terms, corporate governance describes how best to direct and control an organization. An expanded description would be the systems and frameworks outlining the rules, relationships, and processes within and by which authority is exercised and controlled in corporations.

A central component of governance is the assembling of directors in boards to act as agents on behalf of owners. To minimize potential for agency costs, agents are expected to act in the best interest of the organization, avoid conflicts of interest, and not misuse their position or the information to which they have privileged access. More specifically, they are to prevent insolvent trading and expected to disclose related party transactions and their interests.

Agents, moreover, are bound by behavioral expectations associated with the business judgment rule. This effectively stipulates that the law does *not* intend to inhibit proper entrepreneurial activity, but directors must meet set judgment requirements for care and diligence:

- Make the judgment in good faith, for a proper purpose.
- Do not have material personal interest in the subject matter of the judgment.
- Inform themselves about the subject matter to the reasonable extent they believe appropriate.
- Rationally believe that the judgment is in the best interests of the corporation.

The resource-based view, covered in Part I, relies on family input to properly establish "familiness" resources. Similarly, governors and directors, whether family or external, need a working understanding of the resources available that are idiosyncratic, to enable them to guide the bundling that builds unique capability, which drives strategic planning and sustained differentiation and performance. Family owners, therefore, have a responsibility to:

- Clearly define values,
- Clarify stakeholder priorities,
- Provide shared vision,
- Set shareholder goals, and
- Assure unity and commitment.

Familial Meta-Framework: Business Governor – Family Governor

Business governors are expected to oversee business *performance* and ensure *conformance* with legal frameworks. Their decisions are bound by a set of rules and objectives contained in a document known as a constitution, previously a "memorandum and articles of association." However, how this is termed may depend on the jurisdiction. The company's constitution is a contract between the shareholders and the company, and each person who applies to be a shareholder or member of the company agrees to abide by the documented rules.

Business governors (i.e. directors), moreover, understand that their duty is to the company, not to the constituency they represent. This sentence and notion is important; read it again. This also relates to the family governors, though it is not legally binding in the family context.

Directing the business or the family requires mastering independent thinking and judgment. Go ahead and read that again as well. Then, consider asking yourself and others this question: "to whom are you accountable?"

When making decisions, governors abide by a set of parameters, which were captured eloquently by the King Commission (King 2002):

- Is there any conflict?
- Do I have all the facts to enable me to make a decision?
- Is this a rational decision based on all the facts?
- Is the decision in the best interests of the company?
- Is the communication to stakeholders transparent?
- Is the organization acting in a socially responsible way?
- Am I a good steward of the organization's assets?
- Would the board be embarrassed if its decision and the process employed in arriving at its decision appeared on the front page of a national newspaper?

Considering that there is more than one type of board is important. They range from passive to active. Passive boards meet minimal requirements and can be often described as cosmetic. Active boards at a minimum provide oversight (i.e. overseeing those who do), and, ideally, are full blown decision-making forums. Related to strategy, they need to establish (i) arenas: where will we be active? (ii) vehicles: how we are going to do it? (iii) differentiation: how we will be seen to be different? (iv) staging: what will be the speed and the sequence of moves? and (v) economic logic: how does what we do translate into financial terms?

In addition to strategy, the board has a role in crafting the mission. This involves (i) establishing a focused conceptual approach (i.e. the what), (ii) the meaning of what it is we do (i.e. the why; the noble purpose), and (iii) the plausible chances of success (i.e. the aspirational goals).

Some insightful boards steer their constituents away from mission statements to rather concentrate on "commitment statements." Such commitment statements can vary for different stakeholders, e.g. employees, customers, family, and owners. The additional granularity of this contextual approach is obvious and meaningful.

Individual Meta-Framework: Four Tests Framework

Any individual strategizing their career—or involvement—in the family or the business needs to be comfortable with that which distinguishes family businesses from others. When (not if) asked by an independent, objective evaluator how they see the differences, rather than shoot from the hip they should be prepared with an evidence-based answer. More specifically, a strong response could sound like this: "The competitive advantages that family enterprises have over others, according to research, include their speed to market, which stems from their concentrated ownership that leads to efficient decision-making and response time. They are also more likely to have an intentional strategic focus on niches. Their characteristic long-term perspective ensures a commitment to quality. They invest patient capital and are renowned for their agility and flexibility and typically enjoy lower overall cost structures."

A response like that is the tool of the trade for anyone serious about contributing to this domain. It is also something that an external director should understand, particularly those with a publicly traded company pedigree.

If you are a candidate seeking a governance role, consider responding with what the research says about best-practice governed family businesses. A version of this should do it: "In award-winning family business, that is, those who are considered best-practice in governance terms, shareholders act as long-term proprietors.

The board is deeply invested, which means they are motivated to undertake disciplined monitoring of financial and non-financial results. The CEO is typically compensated mostly via long-term incentives. That person is usually an insider who has considerable experience and a list of substantive accomplishments. The CEO is values- and mission-driven and typically stays in the job for decades. That executive is supported by a top management team with a strong voice and diverse functional backgrounds, with members who are multigenerational and enjoy long tenures. The leadership's philosophy is centered on careful stewardship over the mission as well as assets and resources. They have a reputation for being willing to listen and invest in capabilities to enhance prospects of long-term success."

Enough said!

Generational Meta-Framework: Learn Our Family Business

Many of the current popular corporate governance practices may be detrimental to family businesses in that they may harm family unity, might be too complex for private firms, and/or are applicable only to very large, public companies with dispersed ownership. This reinforces the need to spend time in L2 of the Four Ls: learn our family business. It is here that the next generation can understand their family business governance needs and design the appropriate governance architecture, in consultation with incumbents and advisors. It is during this time that they will appreciate that which is different not only with regard to their family business, but for family business writ large. Specifically, they will come to know the importance of being accountable, or the need to justify decisions made and accept responsibility for their implementation. This accountability will entail avoiding conflicts between family members' roles in the family and business, while preserving an atmosphere of trust and unity.

In L2, there is a need to understand risk, as that will be fundamental to individuals' ability to lead (as expected in L3). They will need to review the business's risk appetite, consider structures for risk management, establish measures to supervise risk, introduce ways to implant risk into governance, and design crisis management protocols. Remember the board is responsible for supervising risk while management is responsible for managing risk.

One recommendation is that these family leaders will need to champion, if not already in place, the introduction of external directors to the board. This will have many benefits and contribute significantly to continuity. Call them "externals" rather than independents, because anyone sitting on the board should be an independent thinker. These externals bring value through their unbiased, objective views. Not being mired in historical influences on the company or family, they bring fresh broad perspectives. As well, they bring a network of contacts and, because of their non-operational role, they are more likely to hold management accountable for their actions.

When asked if there is one thing that a family can do to increase their chances of continuity, pioneer family enterprise scholar Professor Emeritus John Ward will reply, "Appoint externals to the board." When asked "How many?" he will answer, "Minimum of three." When further probed regarding "How many family?" he'll say, "It doesn't matter as long as there are three externals." Admittedly, it is a bit more complicated than that, but I include this idea to add gravitas to the importance of getting this done while in L2.

A good way to frame what value an external brings to the discourse is to consider that they don't tell, they ask. Their role, often times, is to "cause you to pause," and be more deliberate in making decisions. Jim Ethier, the Emeritus Chairman at A.H. Bush and Co., explained it well when he shared that "a board is like the group of consulting physicians grouped around a hospital bed considering prognosis and best procedures for a patient. They arrive to consensus when all relevant information and perspectives are shared. They also do this in a timely fashion, acting with a sense of urgency not a sense of panic." He also stresses that gender mix is important in order to capture the gamut of perspectives.

Tactical Meta-Framework: Governance – The Governor

The board needs to understand, test, and endorse the business strategy. While some boards adopt a traditional approach whereby management develops the strategy for board approval, a contemporary approach sees the board shape the direction and drive performance in collaboration with management.

Regardless, a governor (director) has legal duties, which will be a version of five things:

- A duty to act with due care and diligence.
- A duty to act in good faith.
- A duty not to gain advantage by improper use of the position.
- A duty not to misuse information.
- A duty not to trade while insolvent.

The governor contributes to the board, which is responsible as a group for ensuring the creation of long-term sustainable value. As part of this responsibility, directors appoint and oversee the CEO, who recruits management to carry out day-to-day activities within the framework of policies and strategic guidelines established by the board. The top executive is also responsible for making resources available to management to achieve the strategic plan.

The chairperson's governor role is more important than many realize. To some, the chairperson's role is as a figurehead, but in reality, it is to ensure the board functions optimally. The chairperson does this by assuming responsibility for six things:

- The board's general performance,

- The flow of financial information to the board,

- The establishment and maintenance of systems to facilitate the flow of information to the board,

- Public announcement of information,

- Maintenance of cash reserves and group solvency, and

- Making recommendations to the board as to prudent management.

In the corporate governance world, the board is the ultimate decision-maker. Each member of the board is held individually accountable for the outcome. The chairperson manages the process but is not alone in being responsible for the quality of debate. Leaving footprints in the sand is recommended. That means establishing a pathway for how decisions are made, which could include (i) collecting and assessing relevant data, (ii) identifying and framing the primary issue(s), and (iii) bringing others along.

Being a governor requires a heightened tolerance of ambiguity. Decisions are made with imperfect information. That is just the way it is. But it is the director's responsibility to structure their questioning. A template could include five items:

- Have we been presented with adequate information?

- Will the key assumptions hold up?

- What will the competitors' response be?

- What is the risk involved and the penalty in case of error?

- Are the more common points of project failure covered?

Fundamental Meta-Framework: Renewal – Business-Driven Capabilities

Governing for continuity may involve a different approach to that pursued to date. Governors in a continuity paradigm may need to address ingrained habits related to several areas:

- Secretive traits that can affect compensation systems, incentives, information systems.

- Organizational habits developed during the entrepreneurial stage that inhibit strategic renewal and change.

- An ingrained tendency for quick decision-making.

- Culture that may be more oriented to the personality of the leaders than to the requirements of strategy.

- A next generation that struggles to gain organizational power and respect necessary to successfully implement strategies.

Any review of governance effectiveness could include four areas and related questions:

- *Board composition:* Does the Board have the right people and structures in place?

- *Governance relations:* Are the members of the governance system (board, CEO, company secretary) interacting constructively?

- *Internal processes:* How efficiently does the board manage governance processes such as meetings, information flows, and others?
- *Stakeholder communications:* How effectively does the board communicate with its key stakeholders?

Family Governance

Keystone Meta-Framework: Family Steward

Recall the four ways that costs can be incurred when agents are not stewards: entrenchment, altruism, adverse selection, and information asymmetry. This applies equally to family and non-family. So, it's critical to understand these four potential costs and that good governance is what reduces their potential impact. Revisit this to strategically and comprehensively craft your family's governance philosophy.

Familial Meta-Framework: Sense of Purpose

The real purpose of committing to governance in the family, the ownership, or the business systems is to demonstrate a commitment to family unity that motivates the collective to be effective owners and to support their businesses for the long term.

Individual Meta-Framework: Political

Governing an increasingly diverse family of families is likely to be politically charged. Knowing that there are differences should drive the development of role clarity and transparency through governance initiatives. As Ward maintains, "you govern a family like you cook a small fish. . .gently."

Generational Meta-Framework: Learn to Lead

The Four Ls applies to both governance roles and operational roles. So, follow the Ls. L1: learning business is a prerequisite for any governing role in business or family. L2: learning our family business is non-negotiable for governors. L3: learning to lead will help to govern our family business. L4: learning to let go any governance role (not just operational role) is important.

The message that one family took away from interpreting the Four Ls is that "each generation needs to *conquer* the business. . .and a lot of what is required to do that happens in the second L."

Tactical Meta-Framework: Four Rs

One of the Four Rs relates to Remuneration. This is important to address for any governance role. Note that there are two cells of the Four R matrix that must be completed: remuneration for a role as a director and remuneration for a family governance role. The suggestion for the former is to set compensation to market. This is not a universal solution and should be established depending on circumstances. Some families maintain that family directors are already adequately compensated through their dividend and, for those who work in the business, through their salary. So, they don't consider additional compensation for governance roles appropriate. Fair enough. Others take the opposite perspective and set compensation for any director role and related committee activity at market rate. Again, fair enough. Both can work. But there is a need to be transparent. Some opt for taking compensation for governance roles but direct it to philanthropic initiatives, for example. A win-win solution. Regardless, there is a need to understand the other two Rs (requirements and responsibility) for the *role* as governor.

The second role as a family member, again, does not come with a universal remuneration solution. A common approach is to compensate for special project work or leadership roles, but not for other roles. Other incentives such as being able to attend education programs and conferences can be attractive. Whatever the approach, it should be clearly articulated in the family protocol or some such document. One thing that can be expected is that voluntary family governance roles are fatiguing and keeping levels of motivation high becomes problematic. This is normal. Creating meaningful roles with appropriately meaningful compensation is an ongoing challenge.

Fundamental Meta-Framework: Trust

Recall, the aim of the game is to build trust within, between, and among a team of decision-making teams. *Within* the different boards (business, family, ownership, foundation), *between* each of these in dyads (business–family, business–ownership, business–foundation, family–ownership, family–foundation, ownership–foundation), and *among* the business, family, ownership and foundation boards. Revisit the trust dimensions i.e. Integrity, Ability, Benevolence and Consistency.

Ownership Governance

Keystone Meta-Framework: Owner–Stewards

As in all governance roles, owners–stewards are expected to fulfill compliance and performance roles. To external stakeholders, they provide accountability and oversee the formation of strategy. For internal stakeholders they are required to monitor and provide oversight and make policy.

Governing for continuity requires developing a hybrid approach, which mixes some aspects of the market model of governance with some from the control approach. Consider that the market model prescribes high levels of disclosure, independent board members, shareholders who view their holding as one of many assets they hold, and that ownership and management are separate. These are blended with control-model components including a focus on long-term strategy, shareholders who have connections other than financial (i.e. as executives and board members), where ownership and management can overlap significantly.

Familial Meta-Framework: Four Ps — Protocols Before Needed

While not relevant *only* for ownership governance, this is as good a place as any to consider how board processes can be established and improved. One thing that may be apparent is that no matter whether we are governing the business, family, ownership, or foundation, for continuity there are some practices to which we should consistently adhere. So, in the spirit of putting in the protocols (practices) in places before they are needed, what are those practices? Here are key items of consideration as you craft your family's governance philosophy.

As far as meetings, a good rule of thumb is that "more is more," at least initially: err on the side of scheduling more frequent meetings until there is a level of comfort with the discipline of formal meetings. Eventually, the recommendation for business meetings is four to six per year. The reasoning is that management will have time between meetings to have acted on any directive from the board. In other words, leave time between meetings to avoid having to discuss the same topics at each.

For meeting duration and timing, half-day meetings are preferred, and many prefer holding them on Mondays: or at least early in the week. The idea is to allocate time on the preceding weekend to preparation. That means distributing minutes and agendas with ample time to facilitate preparation. One board retreat per year, if possible, is also recommended.

It's ideal to have the business board, family board, ownership board, and foundation board meet in the same week four times a year. This will of course mean multiple meetings for those who occupy multiple roles. But the efficiency of setting a calendar like this outweighs any inconvenience or perception of workload. The work still must be done. This also means that informal gatherings can be scheduled at the same time, so that family members can connect with each other, along with externals, management, and advisors.

As noted above, agendas must be designed carefully and distributed in advance. Put more bluntly, a meeting without a thoughtfully constructed agenda is a waste of time. I'll say it again: a meeting without a thoughtfully constructed agenda is a waste of time. A well-designed agenda aids the flow of information and shapes subsequent discussion for any board. It directs attention to what is important. Before the meeting, it guides preparation. During the meeting, it acts as an objective control of progress, given how quickly things can get off-track. Afterward, the agenda serves as a measure of meeting success. Indeed, you know when the meeting has been effective and efficient; it's typically because the agenda was well thought through and the chairperson aligned discussion with the agenda's roadmap.

Similarly, board papers are art. These critical documents should include the agenda; minutes from previous meetings; major correspondence; CEO's (or equivalent's) report including a report on risk/compliance; financial reports; and documentation supporting submissions that require decisions. An easier way to say that is that board papers need to include matters for decision, matters for discussion, and matters for noting, in that order. For fiduciary boards (legal boards) there is a greater expectation of ensuring compliance with governance protocols and following stricter parameters, but the intent should be the same regardless of the type of board. A trap that

187

some boards fall into is spending so much time complying with legislated protocols that no substantive discussion takes place. Beware this trap. Or the inverse of that, where there is a lack of adherence to protocols, and it becomes a "talk fest" dominated by those with the loudest voices. Either will be a deterrent and a motivator for family members and externals to avoid meaningful participation.

Similarly, the construction of board minutes is an art form. The minutes serve several important functions, such as tracking what happened in the meeting, providing a record for those unable to attend, housing special instructions for committees and others, and representing a permanent record for outside parties that may need to evaluate past decisions. I suggest this is an art form because it is not easy to capture, in detail but parsimoniously, boardroom conversations. Navigating the fine line between including too much and too little information requires skill and practice.

Related to the recommendation to bundle board meetings is the need to design the board calendar, including all aspects of board responsibilities. The calendar will include appropriate interaction with management other than the CEO and ensure that more mundane topics such as insurances review are not overlooked. It will also promote the scheduling of activities in logical order. For example, compensation and remuneration reviews must occur before budget meetings. On the logistical end, attending to this enables synchronization of directors' calendars well in advance and, where possible, scheduling of business-site visits.

At some point, you will need to establish board committees. These save time and increase the efficiency of the board process, while providing a training ground for those moving toward the position of chairperson and enabling faster socialization of new directors. The idea of committees also helps address the question of optimal board size. That is, having a board with seven to ten members facilitates the effective formation of committees that perform meaningful work.

Any fewer members than that will make committee work more onerous and, ultimately, less effective.

Another board-related question relates to tenure. There is no definitive answer, but it's ideal to establish a formal tenure policy. Externals I respect, who have been brought on to provide independent, objective direction, share with me that there is a time after which they feel they are no longer truly independent. One in particular sticks to a five-year rule. After that he is voluntarily out! Broadly, complacency on the board is the enemy, and the frequent cause of discontent and suboptimal performance. Increasingly, the performance of the individual directors and the board as a group are monitored closely and evaluated after each meeting by the directors themselves and annually by an independent auditor. This type of oversight solves many potential problems (those related to agency and principal cost, for example) and can lead to thoughtful replacement of directors. But again, there is no one right way.

Though a renewable appointment is de rigueur, in the first year the new director is still finding their way. Fit is paramount, so it's best to build into the recruitment process a clear way of exiting someone who has been wrongfully appointed. While plenty of consultancies provide board-recruitment services now, it's important not to outsource these conversations fully.

A final observation. Governing requires serious commitment, and good directors are like hen's teeth. Take care to identify, recruit, and retain them.

Individual Meta-Framework: Persuasiveness

The role of a governor, as noted earlier in the book, is "to persuade and be persuadable." Simple. It is worthwhile to include the definition of persuasiveness as it was introduced in the servant leadership framework, but with changing the word "leaders" to governors, as below.

Persuasive mapping (persuasiveness) describes the extent to which governors use sound reasoning and mental frameworks. Governors high in persuasive mapping are skilled at mapping issues and conceptualizing greater possibilities as well as being compelling when articulating these opportunities. They encourage others to visualize the organization's future and commit to bringing the vision to life; they are never coercive or manipulative.

Generational Meta-Framework: Sibling Partnership

The four ownership stages framework provided a way to understand the ownership trajectory. Extending that, it is important to acknowledge that there are different types of owners (recall the ownership circle of the three circles framework). These include operating owners, governing owners, active owners, investing owners, and passive owners. The emphasis and mix of types are typically a function of the generation in question. Regardless, owners have four broad responsibilities (with actions in the bullet points):

1. To define the values that shape the company's culture.

   • Regular meetings and sessions between owners and managers.

2. To set the vision.

   • Establish parameters and boundaries for management strategies.

   • Integrate business strategic planning with family values.

3. To specify financial targets.

   • Owners propose goals for growth, risk, liquidity, and profitability; the board evaluates feasibility and consistency.

4. To elect the directors and design the board.

- Appoint active and independent directors.

Tactical Meta-Framework: Responsibility

The best way, arguably, to start the family governance journey is to populate the four Rs matrix. This will evolve into the family constitution (also known as the family protocol or family charter).

Family constitutions provide the parameters that govern the relationships among owners, family members, and managers. These documents make explicit some of the principles and guidelines that owners will follow in their relations with each other, other family members, and managers. It is an important contributor to family unity.

There are plenty of resources to guide the drafting of a family constitution, and literally thousands of "experts" occupy this space. It is recommended that the experts are engaged to keep the process on track, but not to write the document. This one belongs to the family. Keep in mind, also, that the *process* is important. Do not rush the process just to produce a document, to tick a box. What's created if you don't commit seriously will more than likely be meaningless and end up gathering dust on a shelf somewhere. Make it a living document. Understand that no amount of legal expertise can match the goodwill and personal responsibility of family members. The document usually has no legal bearing but can refer to documents that do (e.g. the company constitution, buy-sell agreements, others). Moreover, the development process for a family constitution is a compelling rationale for family meetings and councils in multigenerational family firms.

Anyone who has been through this will reinforce that the process is more important than the document. As part of that process, address the previously "no go" topic areas. You can make up your own list but, on that list, it is advisable to discuss the inclusion of a redemption policy.

Fundamental Meta-Framework: Church

The church represents the family in the church and state framework. Included in the family forums found above the line, in the church, are the family council and family assembly. The family council is the governance body focused on family affairs; it serves the family in a similar way that the board of directors serves the business. It functions to promote communication, provide a forum for resolution of family conflicts, and support the education of next-generation family members and affines.

The family assembly operates in conjunction with the family council, and typically is commissioned when the family becomes too large for everyone to participate on the family council. It is another vehicle for education, communication, and the renewal of family bonds. Assemblies are scheduled annually or biannually and provide a way for family members to engage meaningfully, either in the planning and implementation or through active participation.

The Foundation

Keystone Meta-Framework: Social

The family's foundation is the vehicle through which to deliver on the social-logic-driven initiatives in the two logics framework. It emerges, typically, in multigenerational families as wealth accumulates or as a consequence of a liquidity event such as the sale of a legacy asset. The foundation's role is significant in ensuring long-lasting, impactful societal contributions. While likely bound by legal and structures, there is an expectation that the organization will be governed with the same formality of the business, with a clear strategy, requisite accountability, and transparency, along with the inclusion of external directors.

Familial Meta-Framework: Big Tent—Philanthropy

The foundation is a way to engage family members, both lineal and affines, in the family-owning business ecosystem. The proviso is that there be a clear pathway to make people ready, willing, and capable to contribute in a meaningful way. As such, allocating someone a role in the foundation to park them somewhere with an inflated salary and dubious key performance indicators is counter to what the *Continuity Model Generation* supports. Don't be tempted. Don't.

Individual Meta-Framework: Empathy and Altruism

While having a business understanding is required, this will likely be complemented by the servant leadership dimensions of altruism and empathy. It is worth listing all five again with a shift in emphasis, as below.

Wisdom can be understood as a combination of awareness of surroundings and anticipation of consequences. The combination of these two characteristics makes governors adept at picking up cues from the environment and understanding their implications. Governors high in wisdom are characteristically observant and anticipatory across most functions and settings.

Emotional healing (empathy) describes a governor's commitment to and skill in fostering spiritual recovery from hardship or trauma. Governors using emotional healing are highly empathetic and great listeners, making them adept at facilitating the healing process. Governors create environments that are safe for employees to voice personal and professional issues. Moreover, followers who experience personal traumas will turn to governors high in emotional healing.

Altruistic calling (altruism) describes a governor's deep-rooted desire to make a positive difference in others' lives. It is a generosity of the spirit consistent with a philanthropic purpose in life. Because the ultimate goal is to serve, leaders high in altruistic calling will put others' interests ahead of their own and will work diligently to meet followers' needs.

Persuasive mapping (persuasiveness) describes the extent to which governors use sound reasoning and mental frameworks. Governors high in persuasive mapping are skilled at mapping issues, conceptualizing greater possibilities, and are compelling when articulating these opportunities. They encourage others to visualize the organization's future and commit to bringing the vision to life; they are never coercive or manipulative.

Organizational stewardship describes the extent to which governors prepare an organization to make a positive contribution to society through community development, programs, and outreach. Organizational stewardship involves an ethic or value for taking responsibility for the well-being of the community and ensuring that the strategies and decisions undertaken reflect the commitment to give back and leave things better than found. They also work to develop a community spirit in the workplace, one that facilitates leaving a positive legacy.

Generational Meta-Framework: Crazy Quilt

The crazy quilt applies to the family foundation. Pivoting from a purely business focus to a more socially focused agenda will likely mean that those "quilters" have a broader, more diverse worldview. Their passion will be about driving positive societal change. Harnessing this passion and complementing and balancing it with commercial nous is not as challenging as it once was. This is a result of the legitimization of social entrepreneurship and impact investing.

The other three principles of effectuation can similarly be applied to the socially anchored agendas of the family foundation. They still need to understand the resources they have at their disposal (bird-in-the-hand), be risk-savvy (affordable loss), and be able to pivot appropriately (lemonade principle).

Tactical Meta-Framework: Customer

The BSC reminds us of the importance of customers. Those charged with governing the foundation need to understand their customers and how demographics influence change. A recent example is the current, fast-moving trend away from previously established norms related to social issues. Current generations, moreover, tend to focus philanthropically more on the sciences and less on the arts than in the past. Also, a clear understanding of partnership arrangements is paramount.

Increasingly, foundations understand the need for sound metrics. Causes that provide little in the way of auditable reporting and accountability are likely not the customer preferred by professionally governed foundations. Several key questions go a long way to remove charlatans and opportunists from the foundation's preferred partner/customer list: Who is the customer? What is their track record? How are they governed? Are there recent testimonials and evidence of performance metrics?

Fundamental Meta-Framework: Business-Driven Capabilities

The understanding that the foundation *is* a business should drive all discussion. ENOUGH SAID.

Part III

Configuring a Plan for the Plans

Configuration Plan One

The first option would be to consider each of the four plans with their four components of the Continuity Canvas equally. And plan to complete each of the quadrants in some equitable and methodical way. This is commendable but not recommendable.

The reason for this is that some of the work will have already be complete. Another reason would be that a lot depends on the urgency, which is influenced by the life cycle of the business, the family stage of the family, and the sophistication of the ownership group. This may not be the most efficient way to proceed. It is however a test of the map components. And a great reference point.

Moving the quadrants of the canvas to fit the story line is a simple but effective way to capture the many different storylines. First you need to master the four plans and four dimensions.

After attempting to configure as individuals, get together with others to discuss and decide. Then, perhaps, move forward on crafting each cornerstone concept.

This is also the opportunity to test your knowledge and understanding of the *Continuity Model Generation* approach. This is included here rather than earlier because the robustness, for want of a better word, which is a proxy for sustainability of your nuanced approach, will be contingent on how best you comprehend the richness of the 21 frameworks and the embedded 87 dimensions. Importantly, there is no need to know these in any detail. Knowing that the canvas that you build is developed on a solid foundation of theory-driven, evidenced-based frameworks is important. Don't fall into the trap of rushing to know "how" to do it. . .that is not sustainable. Rather, have the discipline to appreciate that the simplicity of the Continuity Canvas masks its complexity.

At this point it is assumed that you are drinking the Continuity Canvas Kool-Aid™ and appreciate the need to think broadly and deeply, while efficiently crafting your idiosyncratic story.

So, spending time with the first configuration is important. Here you will be able to immediately determine that there are four plans with four sub-sections. In the spirit of encouraging you to add your voice, you can call them whatever you are most comfortable with. The four plans can be simplified to be positioned as STRATEGY, TALENT, WEALTH, and GOVERNANCE. Strategy and Governance are to do mainly with the enterprise, while Talent and Wealth are more focused on the individual. The STRATEGIC planning process for continuity has four subsections, principles, or dimensions that contribute to the quadruple bottom-line. While it is your prerogative to change the labels, the foci should still be on financial, social, environmental, and talent in order to maintain the integrity of the Continuity Canvas approach.

The SUCCESSORS' TALENT DEVELOPMENT plan for continuity as presented in the "original" version has four components (call them what you want), which have been proven to best prepare successor generations for business, family, and/or ownership. Again, go ahead and play with the labels, but don't deviate too far from the message that drives each. The way they are presented is broad enough so that you can add your personality, voice, context, situation, or circumstance without needing to change the titles. But, again, the aim is for you to own the story.

You will understand that the ASSET, WEALTH, and ESTATE plan for continuity is intentionally broad and designed to start conversations and careful deliberations. These conversations and deliberations are around legacy, broadly defined. If any of the four plans are most open for interpretation and adaption, it is this one. And this is intentional because it really is personal, with a twist. As each quadrant is introduced in the original configuration, it is effectively more about the who (as in, who is going to be receiving the assets, wealth, and estate). Everyone knows that this is necessary but not sufficient. Focus needs to be concurrently committed to the "why." The "how" comes later and builds off the *why* and the *who* foundations.

The GOVERNANCE plan for continuity is the second of the enterprise plans but it is evident that each of the plans, though independent, are interdependent. Here, again, the four foci are intentional. It may be that, for some, the need for focusing on ownership separately from family is redundant, and that is acknowledged as being the case in many early-stage, generational, business-owning families. Likewise, the Foundation may not be yet formalized. However, don't disregard these as if continuity is something that you will embrace, these will be on the agenda at some point. Herein lies the beauty of this approach. You can configure given the circumstance, as will be shown in the following examples. No need to mess with the labels on this one. Stakeholders will be looking for how you go about planning to govern the business, the ownership, the family, and at some point, the foundation.

So, look again at this four-by-four matrix. Tweak the labels if you feel the need. Then consider the configuration alternative before designing your own plan for the plans.

Configuration Plan One

1a: Financial	1b: Social	2a: Values/History /Legacy	2b: Financial Literacy & Value Creation
1c: Environmental	1d: Talent	2c: Governance Preparation	2d: Individual Development
3a: Family – Nuclear	3b: Family Extended	4a: Business	4b: Family
3c: Other Individuals	3d: Other Groups	4c: Others	4d: Foundation

CONFIGURATION PLAN ONE

Configuration Plan Two

S o, to reinforce, understanding the Continuity Canvas' 16 quadrants is important for 2 reasons. First, it is effectively a language or a code that anyone can use to create their plan for the plans. Second, it allows for multiple configurations.

Take configuration plan two as an example. Here, the configuration story (the plan for the plans) would be that the two enterprise plans, i.e. the STRATEGIC plan and the GOVERNANCE plan, take equal primary priority while the individual plans, i.e. the successors' TALENT development plan and the asset, WEALTH, and estate plan, take equal secondary priority.

Note: The key to the canvas is that the bigger the size of the box, the more attention it needs.

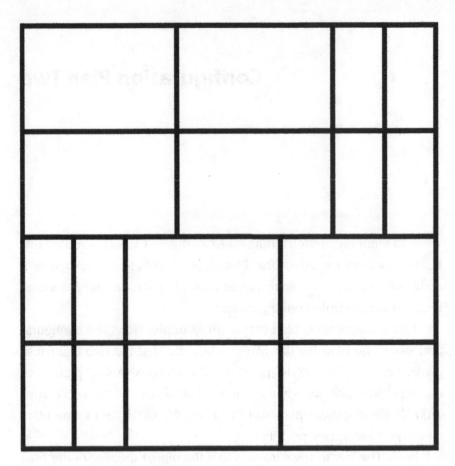

CONFIGURATION PLAN TWO

Configuration Plan Three

In configuration three, the configuration story (i.e. the plan for the plans) would be: The quadrants for the two enterprise plans, i.e. the STRATEGIC plan and the GOVERNANCE plan, are allocated equal priority while the individual plans, i.e. the successors' TALENT development plan and the asset, WEALTH, and estate plan require a more careful approach. The indication is that there is a need for increased *financial literacy* and *governance preparation* for individuals in the successors' talent development planning process. As well, there is attention required to address how *other* individuals fit into the estate, wealth, and asset planning process. Remember, the key to the canvas is that the bigger the size of the box the more attention it needs.

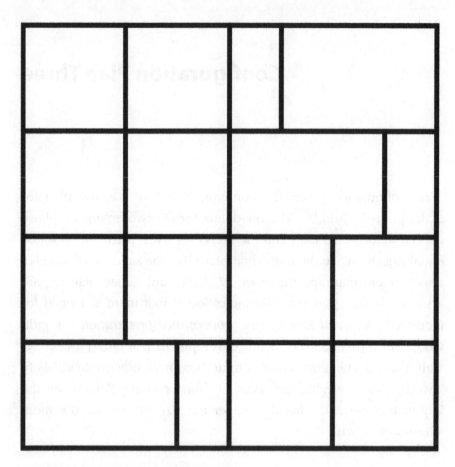

CONFIGURATION PLAN THREE

Continuity Model Generation

Configuration Plan Four

In configuration four, the configuration story (the plan for the plans) is much richer and would be that the quadrants for the STRATEGIC plan indicate that the plan for this plan would be to consider how *social* and *environmental* dimensions complement the already established *financial* and *talent* dimensions. The GOVERNANCE plan matrix suggests that a way forward would be to concentrate on the *business* governance, the *foundation* next, *ownership*, then *family*.

The successors' TALENT developing planning process should look at focusing on *values, history,* and *legacy* education matters as well as programs linked to *individual* development. Then, the more mainstream aspects of *financial literacy* and *governance role* preparation can be established.

Obviously, the configuration combinations are considerable. Going through the process of configuring YOUR Continuity Canvas alone, then with others is an important process. It could be that you decide unanimously to approach the plan for the plans in an agreed-upon order. As in, for example, start with STRATEGY if that is in urgent need, then move onto GOVERNANCE, etc. There is no one way. . .Discuss alternatives, then decide, keeping in mind the inter-dependency message delivered throughout these pages.

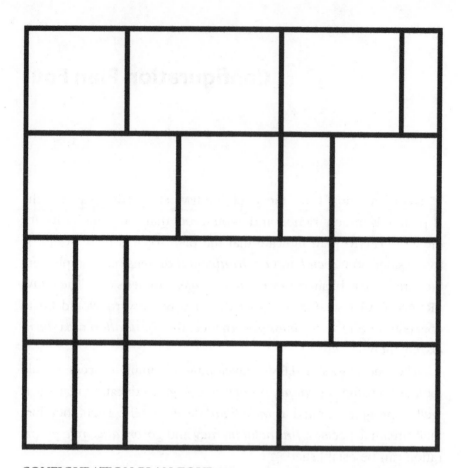

CONFIGURATION PLAN FOUR

But don't make it harder than it needs to be. . .Review the previous sections to ground your approach in the frameworks.

Part IV

Appendix

Educating Educators

Over time, I have come to understand my role to be as an educator of educators. The key is to make the concepts "educatable." If there is any magic in this approach, that's it. That's my magic trick and should be yours.

Readers of this book should now see themselves as educators and, with practice, build competence to educate others. It's my journey to now.

If you are a family member, you educate your siblings, parents, grandparents, children, etc. If you are an advisor, you educate those with whom you work, so that you can educate those you serve. If you are a professor, you should be better equipped to stand in front of your classes and impart the knowledge I have collated here.

Though there are literally thousands of ways to approach the dissemination of the knowledge in these pages, the purpose of this section is to share examples and ideas that may assist in facilitating your own way forward. The fundamental mantra here is that you only truly understand something when you teach it. A supplementary mantra is that you have license to adapt the frameworks but with the caveat that this will only work if you take the time to genuinely understand. *Taking shortcuts is a fool's errand.*

Some things to consider regarding content:

- First, the 21 frameworks have been arranged in the 6 meta-frameworks they have because that is the way that has worked as the concepts and delivery have been tested and re-tested.

Some of the 21 could have been placed in other meta-framework "homes" and some belong in multiple. I would recommend that rather than focus on where you think they belong, use each of the 21 for purpose.

- Second, throughout the book it was stressed that better comprehension eventuates when frameworks are integrated. But this will only happen when each is understood. From experience, there is likelihood that you will gravitate to some frameworks and ignore others. Try not to do this too early.

- Third, don't shy away from the four fundamental theories in the keystone meta-framework. Embrace these.

Here are some useful points that have been developed in unison with the development of the Continuity Canvas:

1. Educating educators: this is a more powerful statement than saying, "you need to be able to understand the concepts so you can teach others." *Educating educators* suggests that the role of the learner is to be able to be confident to educate others who will then educate others, and so on. It fits well with the idea of continuity.

2. Mindset/skill set: the idea behind this is that typically we focus on *skill* mastery (i.e. *the how*) and avoid taking the time to consider *the why*. Another way of saying this is, "the doing gets in the way of the thinking." The concepts in this book are intentionally designed to move participants toward the "why" end of the "why–how" continuum.

3. Theory-driven, evidence-based frameworks approach: get used to saying this as each of the 21 frameworks is grounded in this.

4. Content, context, conversations, and constituents: in a paragraph. . . The *content* consists of theory-driven, evidence-based

frameworks that have been stress tested and that make dense complex topics easily digestible, relatable, and learnable. *Context* refers to the idiosyncratic frame of reference that individuals will bring to the concepts. *Conversations* enable the broadening of perspectives, which will deepen the understanding by considering different worldviews. *Constituents* are those in each individual's ecosystem, who will be the people that the newly anointed educator will educate.

5. Theories are lenses that help you make sense of the mess. . . embrace theories: this is vital and needs to be stressed when delivering the keystone meta-framework. Typically, this motivates participants to look for, rather than avoid, theories.

6. Informal formality by design: this refers to the learning culture that should be developed. This is enhanced through (i) buzz sessions to discuss concepts (dyads or triads), (ii) breakout groups of more than three but less than ten to interpret concepts and apply them with different perspectives, (iii) living cases are the extremely rich learnings provided by visitors to class sessions to share their experience, (iv) continuous application to the instructor's personal experience or reference to case examples of which they preferably have first-hand experience, and (v) the revisiting of concepts, which refers to the need to loop back and not consider each framework in isolation.

7. Each framework and meta-framework is independent but interdependent: this is crucial. There would be a natural tendency to look at each framework in isolation. Best is to deliver each separately and look for ways they "hang together." As an example, consider how the four Ls framework is enhanced when you include the four Rs and the "Four Tests of a Prince" in the two first Ls ("learning business" and "learning our family

213

business") and then look at referring to the four exit strategies when explaining the transition from L3 ("learning to lead") and L4 ("learning to let go"). Another example could be to look at interpreting the four Ls through an agency theoretical (from the keystone meta-framework). This would be a way to understand entrenchment (L3 and L4). This is not difficult; it just takes time (to understand) and practice (in delivery).

8. Add your voice: this is important and something I found out slowly. Some self-disclosure here. I struggled trying to imitate my mentors Professors Emeriti Ken Moores and John Ward. It was only when I abandoned that strategy and made the concepts my own that I was able to really make a difference. This relates to a key learning from L2 (and this will not be the first time you have heard this): "keep the philosophies not the detail. . . in order to continue differently." If I hadn't been able to do this, I would have left academe. . . frustrated. So, own the concepts and tell the story in a way that is most comfortable for you.

9. Stress that framework thinking enables being able to have difficult conversations easily. Understand and reinforce that the shared end game is to continue differently. Another more powerful message is that the underlying notion of the *Continuity Model Generation* is to pursue an unattainable mission. And the secret to achieving this is through integrating *old* ideals with *new* ideas.

10. The illustrations provided are gold. Stress that opportunities to educate others will not always be in classroom settings. It is likely that most of the time they won't be. Use the idea of being able to replicate the concepts on coasters or napkins, because there is a good chance that you will be in arm's length of a coaster and/or a napkin when a learning opportunity presents itself.

Educating Educators

A Program Example

Part One: Frameworks and Meta-Frameworks

	Preamble	Focus
Introduction	As well as an opportunity for each participant to share their circumstance, this session will include information about "the approach." Specifically, related to mindset/skill set; theories as lenses; theory-driven, evidence-based frameworks; 21-87-6; 4×4	Sharing the process and the destination is important. The destination is designing *YOUR* Continuity Canvas built on four foci: • STRATEGY, • TALENT, • WEALTH, and • GOVERNANCE.
Keystone Meta-framework	With knowledge of this meta-framework's keystone four theoretical approaches, two logics, and three circles, anyone will be able to understand and interpret with some authority the complexity of the tripartite business, ownership, and family landscape as well as how they function independently and interdependently.	This session will set the tone around appreciating the need to embrace "lenses," i.e. theory-driven, evidence-based frameworks. The dimensions of each of these frameworks are easily digestible and universally applicable. A special emphasis will be placed on ensuring that the concepts come to life by including real examples from "exemplars."

(Continued)

Fundamental Meta-framework	Clarity around, and commitment to, the four frameworks that make up the fundamental meta-framework is paramount. Without this clarity and commitment, the other five meta-frameworks will likely not gain traction.	This session will introduce the importance of TRUST (within, between, and among a team of decision-making teams). Understanding life cycles will also be described, as well as some foundational entrepreneurship concepts (e.g. entrepreneurial orientation and effectuation). Innovation capabilities and a fundamental way to look at business and ownership governance (church and state framework) will be introduced.
Tactical Meta-framework	Being tactically savvy requires a clear understanding of how and why you are where you are as well as what and who is going to get the business, the owners, and the family across upcoming chasms.	The focus of this session will be strategy mapping. As well as core business activities, the importance of strategically planning for other commercial activities in addition to personal lives and family will be included. Managing different types of risk will be covered. Considering how to accommodate the diverse expectations of stakeholders in the entrepreneurship ecosystem will be interwoven.

(Continued)

Individual Meta-framework	The 16 dimensions that make up the 4 frame-works of the Individual meta-framework consider the gamut of questions that all will need to answer at some point in their life's journey. Most, if not all, relate to roles removed from any in the business, such is their richness.	In this session, the focus will center around the individual and set the scene for participants to consider their personal philosophies of leadership and consider the difficul-ties of letting go as well as start to think about exit strategies and legacy.
Familial Meta-framework	The four frameworks that make up the Familial meta-framework ensure that having difficult con-versations is substantially simpler.	In this session, the frameworks are consid-ered to have contributed significantly to assist-ing multigenerational, business-owning families continue across generations.
Generational Meta-framework	The 12 dimensions of the Generational meta-framework forces reflection on the circum-stances that surround now and next genera-tions. It focuses on the understanding that what got you here won't get you where it is you want and need to be.	This session provides additional luster to the conversations sparked in the familial meta-framework session.

Part Two: Four Plans and Cornerstone Concepts for Continuity

	Preamble	Process
Strategy Strategic Planning for Continuity Strategic Planning for the Continuity Cornerstone Concept: Design a Quadruple Bottom-Line Scorecard.	Knowing where you are, where you want to go to, and deciding from among the options the best way to get there is the best way to look at strategic planning. Simple is best. But the simplicity masks the complexity. Deciding on objectives, measures, and targets sounds easier than it is. And then consider that you need to do this for operating businesses, liquid assets, real estate holdings, and philanthropic activities. Deciding who is going to do what by when is crucial and important. . . But integrating multiple strategic plans is exponentially complex.	1. List all commercial activities for which strategic planning is required. 2. Rank the list from the top priority to the least important. 3. Evaluate how robust the strategic planning process is for the commercial activities on a crude scale (e.g., from 10 (is adequate) to 1 (desperately needs work)). A picture will present itself. 4. Plan to establish objectives, measures, and targets for the 4 "bottom-line" categories using concepts from the 21 frameworks.

(Continued)

(Continued)

Talent	Preparing the right people, the right way takes careful planning. . . and pivoting. The end game is a talent pool of all-rounders with complementary skill sets and mindsets to tackle increasingly complex environments. But just as environments are increasingly complex, so too, it seems, are individuals.	1. Make a list of who's who in the zoo (family tranch, age, education, work experience, etc.)
Family Talent Development Planning for the Continuity Cornerstone Concept: Develop an Informed Individual Philosophy of Stewardship.		2. Begin a development plan for the list, including incumbent leadership.
		3. Meet individually. Consider testing instruments for younger members of the cohort. Establish an education budget.
		4. Divide into 4 education and preparation focused categories; populate each using concepts from the 21 frameworks.

(Continued)

Wealth Asset, Wealth, and Estate Planning for the Continuity Cornerstone Concept: Produce a Handwritten Personal Legacy Statement.	Continuing in the best financial shape is the Holy Grail. Everyone knows that. . . But most postpone doing anything about it. . . Until it is too late. Much hinges on this plan, which is arguably the most important of the four.	1. Review the ownership system to establish by category what is owned. 2. Look at the ownership with additional granularity by establishing ownership by % for key assets. 3. Establish the vehicles that hold the ownership, e.g. personal, family partnership, or trusts. 4. Divide into 4 recipient categories and populate each using concepts from the 21 frameworks.

(Continued)

(Continued)

Governance	Governing the grow-	1. Research what
Governance Planning	ing family group, the	others do. . . Look
for the Continuity	heterogeneous owner-	at families at the
Cornerstone Concept:	ship group as well as	next stage for
Craft the Family's Gov-	the array of operating	your family.
ernance Philosophy.	and investment entities	2. Prioritize what
	requires planning and	needs to be
	oversight.	governed (e.g.
		business, fam-
		ily, ownership,
		foundation)
		3. Begin to discover
		who needs to
		be prepared or
		approached to
		fill governance
		positions.
		4. Divide into 4 gov-
		ernance categor-
		ies and populate
		each using con-
		cepts from the 21
		frameworks.

Part Three: Presenting Configuration Examples

Plan Example	Details
Configuration Plan One	This example will focus on the mastery of the four plans and four dimensions.
Configuration Plan Two	In this example, the configuration story (the plan for the plans) is: The two enterprise plans (i.e. STRATEGIC plan and the GOVERNANCE plan) take equal primary priority while the individual plans (i.e. the Successors' Talent development plan and the asset, WEALTH and estate plan) take equal secondary priority.
Configuration Plan Three	In this example, the configuration story would be: The quadrants for the two enterprise plans (i.e. STRATEGIC plan and the GOVERNANCE plan) are allocated equal priority while the individual plans (i.e. the successors' talent development plan and the asset, WEALTH and estate plan) require a more careful approach. The indication is that there is a need for increased *financial literacy* and *governance preparation* for individuals in the successors' talent development planning process. As well, there is attention required to address how *other* individuals fit into the estate, wealth, and asset planning process.

(Continued)

(Continued)

Configuration Plan Four	The configuration four example is much richer and would be delivered as: The quadrants for the STRATEGIC plan indicate that the plan for this plan would be to consider how *social* and *environmental* dimensions complement the already established *financial* and *talent* dimensions. The GOVERNANCE plan matrix suggests that a way forward would be to concentrate on the *business* governance, the *foundation* next, *ownership*, then *family*. The Successors' Talent developing planning process should look at focusing on *values, history,* and *legacy* education matters as well as programs linked to *individual* development. Then, the more mainstream aspects of *financial literacy* and *governance role* preparation can be established.

Part Four: Developing Your Own Continuity Canvas and Cornerstone Concepts

Focus	Detail
Developing a Plan for the Four CONTINUITY CANVAS Plans	The opportunity is now presented to consider how the concepts come together. Participants will have the scope to draft and prepare by having conversations with each other, so they can be better equipped to have conversations with their constituents. Suggestions and directions will be provided.
Crafting Your Four Cornerstone Concepts	Depending on circumstance, participants can include early drafts of their cornerstone concepts.
Evolving into an Enterprising Family / Day Synthesis	Participants will be called upon to share their Continuity Canvas as well as write and share a continuity commitment statement with the cohort.

References and Further Readings

Throughout, I have included thoughts and ideas that have been collected from all sorts of sources for over two decades. Below, I have included the references to those that have been actually mentioned in the book as well as many others that I encourage readers to consider accessing. Any oversight is mine.

References

Barbuto Jr, J.E. and Wheeler, D.W. (2006). Scale development and construct clarification of servant leadership. *Group & Organization Management*, 31(3), 300–326.

Barney, J. (1991). Firm resources and sustained competitive advantage. *Journal of Management*, 17(1), 99–120.

Bierly, P.E., Kessler, E.H., and Christensen, E.W. (2000). Organizational learning, knowledge and wisdom. *Journal of Organizational Change Management*, 13(6), 595–618.

Chandler, A.D. (1990). *Strategy and Structure: Chapters in the History of the Industrial Enterprise* (Vol. 120). MIT Press.

Craig, J.B. and Moores, K. (2017). Leading a Family Business: Best Practices for Long-Term Stewardship. ABC-CLIO.

Craig, J.B. (2017). Leading a family business requires a C-Suite capabilities and an F-Suite mindset. Family Capital Viewpoint, February. http://www.famcap.com/articles/2017/1/31/viewpoint-leading-a-family-business-requires-c-suite-capabilities-and-an-f-suite-mindset (accessed 26 June 2021).

Cray, E. (1978). *Levi's: The 'Shrink-to-Fit' Business that Stretched to Cover the World*. New York: Houghton Mifflin.

Davis, J.H., Schoorman, F.D., and Donaldson, L. (1997). Toward a stewardship theory of management. *Academy of Management Review*, 22(1), 20–47.

Diagnostic and Statistical Manual of Mental Disorders (DSM-5) (2020). American Psychiatric Association.

Dietz, G. and Den Hartog, D.N. (2006). Measuring trust inside organisations. *Personnel Review*, 35(5), 557–588.

Dyer, D. and Gross, D. (2001). *The Generations of Corning*. New York: Oxford University Press.

Goshen, Z. and Squire, R. (2010). Principal costs: A new theory for corporate law and governance. *Columbia Law Review*, 117, 767–830.

Greenleaf, R.K. (1977). *Servant Leadership: A Journey into the Nature of Legitimate Power and Greatness*. New York: Paulist Press.

Habbershon, T.G. and Williams, M.L. (1999). A resource-based framework for assessing the strategic advantages of family firms. *Family Business Review*, 12(1), 1–25.

Johnson, S.C. (1988). *The Essence of a Family Enterprise*. Indiana: Curtis Publishing Co.

Kaplan, R.S. and Norton, D.P. (1992). The balanced scorecard: Measures that drive performance. *Harvard Business Review*, 71–79.

Kaplan, R.S. and Norton, D.P. (1996). *The Balanced Scorecard: Translating Strategy into Action*. Boston, MA: Harvard Business School Publishing.

Kaplan, R.S. and Norton, D.P. (2001). The strategy-focused organization. *Strategy and Leadership*, 29(3), 41–42.

King. (2002). King Report on Corporate Governance for South Africa. www.mervynking.co.za/downloads/CD_King2.pdf (accessed 25 June 2021).

Lester, D.L., Parnell, J.A. and Carraher, S. (2003). Organizational life cycle: A five-stage empirical scale. *The International Journal of Organizational Analysis*.

Lewicki, R.J. and Bunker, B.B. (1995). Trust in relationships: A model of development and decline. In: *Conflict, Cooperation, and Justice: Essays Inspired by the Work of Morton Deutsch* (eds. B.B. Bunker and J.Z. Rubin), pp. 133–173. San Francisco, CA: Jossey-Bass.

Lewicki, R.J. and Bunker, B.B. (1996). Developing and maintaining trust in work relationships. In: *Trust in Organizations: Frontiers of Theory and Research,* (eds. R. Kramer and T.R. Tyler). Thousand Oaks, CA: Sage.

Miller, D. and Friesen, P.H. (1984). A longitudinal study of the corporate life cycle. *Management Science*, 30(10), 1161–1183.

Miller, D. and Le Breton-Miller, I. (2005a). *Managing for the Long Run: Lessons in Competitive Advantage from Great Family Businesses*. Boston: Harvard Business School Press.

Miller, D. and Le Breton-Miller, I. (2005b). Management insights from great and struggling family businesses. *Long Range Planning*, 38, 517–530.

Mintzberg, H. (1984). Power and organization life cycles. *Academy of Management Review*, 9(2), 207–224.

Moores, K. and Barrett, M. (2003). *Learning Family Business: Paradoxes and Pathways*. (2002) Ashgate Publishing Limited, UK. Reprinted (2010) Bond University Press.

Moores, K.J. and Craig, J.B. (2006). From vision to variables: A scorecard to continue the professionalization of a family firm. In: *Handbook of Research on Family Business*. Elgar Publications, pp. 196–214.

Sirmon, D.G. and Hitt, M.A. (2003). Managing resources: linking unique resources, management, and wealth creation in family firms. *Entrepreneurship Theory and Practice*, 27, 339–358.

Tomer, J.F. (2001). Understanding high-performance work systems: the joint contribution of economics and human resource management. *The Journal of Socio-Economics*, 30(1), 63–73.

Zawislak, P.A., Cherubini Alves, A., Tello-Gamarra, J. et al. (2012). Innovation capability: from technology development to transaction capability. *Journal of Technology Management & Innovation*, 7(2), 14–27.

Further Readings

Ackoff, R. (1978). *The Art of Problem Solving: Accompanied by Ackoff's Fables*. New York: Wiley.

Adizes, I. (2004). *Managing Corporate Lifecycles*. The Adizes Institute Publishing.

Aronoff, C.E. and Ward, J.L. (2011). Family Business Values: *How to Assure a Legacy of Continuity and Success*. Palgrave Macmillan.

Aronoff, C.E. and Ward, J.L. (2011). *Make Change Your Family Business Tradition*. Palgrave Macmillan.

Berle, A.A. and Means, G.C. (1932; 1997). *The Modern Corporation and Private Property*. New Brunswick, N. J.

Bork, D., Jaffe, D., Lane, S. et al. (1996). *Working with Family Business*. San Francisco: Jossey-Bass.

COFRA Group. (2017). www.cofraholding.com (accessed 7 March 2017).

Craig, J.B. and Moores, K. (2002). How Australia's Dennis Family Corp. professionalized its family business. *Family Business Review*, 15(1), 59–70.

Craig, J.B. and Moores, K. (2010). Strategically aligning family and business systems using the Balanced Scorecard. *Journal of Family Business Strategy*, 1(2), 78–87.

Craig, J.B. (2015). Managing the Communication Paradox in the Family Business Circus. Dublin City University, Family Business Centre Ezine, August.

Craig, J.B. (2016). What it takes for a family business to innovate. Kellogg Insight, May. http://insight.kellogg.northwestern.edu/article/what-it-takes-for-a-family-business-to- innovate (accessed 26 June 2021).

Craig, J.B. (2017). The big tent approach. Family Capital Viewpoint, June. http://www.famcap.com/articles/2017/6/27/viewpoint-the-big-tent-approach-being-ready-willing-and-capable-to-contribute-to-family-enterprise (accessed 26 June 2021).

Craig, J.B. (2017). Are your employees putting your company's interest first: a new tool to measure your firm's 'stewardship climate'. Kellogg Insight, February. https://insight.kellogg.northwestern.edu/article/are-your-employees-putting-the-companys-interest-first (accessed 26 June 2021).

Craig, J.B. (2018). Why family businesses sometimes make decisions that seem bad for the family. Kellogg Insight, December.

Danco, L. (1975). *Beyond Survival: A Business Owner's Guide for Success*. Reston, VA: Reston Publishing.

Fraser, J. (2016). *The Handbook of Board Governance: A Comprehensive Guide for Public, Private, and Not-for-Profit Board Members*, (ed. R. Leblanc). Wiley.

Garbuio, M., Lovallo, D. and Sibony, O. (2015). Evidence doesn't argue for itself: the value of disinterested dialogue in strategic decision-making. *Long Range Planning*, 48(6), 361–380.

Greenleaf, R.K. and Spears, L.C. (2002). *Servant Leadership: A Journey into the Nature of Legitimate Power and Greatness*. Paulist Press.

Jaffe, D. (2020). *Borrowed from Your Grandchildren: The Evolution of 100-Year Family Enterprises*. New York: Wiley.

Kaplan, R.S. and Norton, D.P. (2004). *Strategy Maps: Converting Intangible Assets into Tangible Outcomes*. Harvard Business Press.

Lansberg, I. (1983). Managing human resources in family firms: the problem of institutional overlap. *Organizational Dynamics*, 12(1), pp. 39–46.

Lansberg, I. (1999). *Succeeding Generations: Realizing the Dream of Families in Business*. Harvard Business Press.

Lansberg, I. (2007). The tests of a prince. *Harvard Business Review*, 85(9), 92–101.

Lumpkin, G.T. and Brigham, K.H. (2011). Long-term orientation and intertemporal choice in family firms. *Entrepreneurship Theory and Practice*, 35(6), 1149–1169.

Lumpkin, G.T. and Dess, G.G. (1996). Clarifying the entrepreneurial orientation construct and linking it to performance. *Academy of Management Review*, 21(1), 135–172.

Miller, D. (1987). Strategy making and structure: Analysis and implications for performance. *Academy of Management Journal*, 30(1), 7–32.

Miller, D. (1993). The architecture of simplicity. *Academy of Management Review*, 18(1), 116–138.

Neubaum, D.O., Dibrell, C., Thomas, C. et al. (2017). Stewardship climate: scale development and validation. *Family Business Review*, 30(1), 37–60. doi: 10.1177/0894486516673701.

Osterwalder, A. and Pigneur, Y. (2010). *Business Model Generation: A Handbook for Visionaries, Game Changers, and Challengers.* Vol. 1. Wiley.

Parris, D.L. and Welty Peachey, J. (2012). Building a legacy of volunteers through servant leadership: A cause-related sporting event. *Nonprofit Management and Leadership*, 23(2), 259–276.

Pendergast, J.M., Ward, J.L. and De Pontet, S.B. (2011). *Building a Successful Family Business Board: A Guide for Leaders, Directors, and Families.* Palgrave Macmillan.

Sarasvathy, S.D. (2009). *Effectuation: Elements of Entrepreneurial Expertise.* Edward Elgar Publishing.

Schulze, W.S., Lubatkin, M.H., Dino, R.N. et al. (2001). Agency relationships in family firms: theory and evidence. *Organization Science*,12, 99–116.

Schulze, W.S., Lubatkin, M.H. and Dino, R.N. (2003). Toward a theory of agency and altruism in family business. *Journal of Business Venturing*, 18, 473–90.

Searle, T.P. and Barbuto, J.E. (2010). Servant leadership, hope, and organizational virtuousness: A framework exploring positive micro and macro behaviors and performance impact. *Journal of Leadership & Organizational Studies*, doi: 10.1177/1548051810383863.

Shockley-Zalabak, P.S., Morreale, S., and Hackman, M. (2010). *Building the High-Trust Organization: Strategies for Supporting Five Key Dimensions of Trust* (Vol. 7). Wiley.

Sirmon, D.G., Hitt, M.A., Ireland, R.D. et al. (2011). Resource orchestration to create competitive advantage: Breadth, depth, and life-cycle effects. *Journal of Management*, 37(5), 1390–1412.

Sonnenfeld, J.A. (1991). *The Hero's Farewell: What Happens When CEOs Retire.* Oxford University Press.

Sonnenfeld, J.A. and Spence, P.L. (1989). The parting patriarch of a family firm. *Family Business Review*, 2(4), 355–375.

Taiguiri, R. and Davis, J.A. (1992). On the goals of successful family companies. *Family Business Review*, 5, 43–62.

Vanneste, B.S., Puranam, P. and Kretschmer, T. (2014). Trust over time in exchange relationships: meta-analysis and theory. *Strategic Management Journal*, 35(12), 1891–1902.

Ward, J.L. (1988). The special role of strategic planning for family businesses. *Family Business Review*, 1(2), 105–117.

Ward, J.L. (1997). Growing the family business: special challenges and best practices. *Family Business Review*, 10(4), 323–337.

Ward, J.L. (2004). *How Governing Family Businesses is Different. Mastering Global Corporate Governance*. Steger, U. (Hrsg.), New York, pp. 135–167.

Ward, J.L. and Aronoff, C.E. (2011). *Preparing Successors for Leadership: Another Kind of Hero*. Macmillan.

Ward, J.L. and Aronoff, C.E. (2011). *Family Business Governance: Maximizing Family and Business Potential*. Macmillan.

Ward, J.L. (2016). *Keeping the Family Business Healthy: How to Plan for Continuing Growth, Profitability, and Family Leadership*. Springer.

Ward, J.L. and Craig, J.B. (2015). Family business succession: 15 guidelines and pathways. Invited article: China, Family Business Report.

Zahra, S.A., Hayton, J.C., Neubaum, D.O. et al. (2008). Culture of family commitment and strategic flexibility: The moderating effect of stewardship. *Entrepreneurship Theory and Practice*, 32(6), 1035–1054.

Zellweger, T.M., Nason, R.S., and Nordqvist, M. (2012). From longevity of firms to transgenerational entrepreneurship of families introducing family entrepreneurial orientation. *Family Business Review*, 25(2), 136–155.

Index